I0048724

HOW TO JUMP-START YOUR WAY TO
REAL ESTATE WEALTH

ROBERT BARBERA

THE **M** MENTORIS PROJECT

The author has made every effort to ensure the accuracy of the information within this book was correct at time of publication. The author does not assume and hereby disclaims any liability to any party for any loss, damage, or disruption caused by errors or omissions, whether such errors or omissions result from accident, negligence, or any other cause.

Mentoris Project
745 South Sierra Madre Drive
San Marino, CA 91108

Copyright © 2022 Mentoris Project
Cover design: Karen Richardson
Cover images: Piven Aleksandr/Shutterstock.com and Yuriy Kulik/Shutterstock.com

More information at www.mentorisproject.org

ISBN: 978-1-947431-54-6
Library of Congress Control Number: 2022949663

All rights reserved, which includes the right to reproduce this book or portions thereof in any form whatsoever except as provided by the U.S. Copyright Law. For information address the Mentoris Project.

All net proceeds from the sale of this book will be donated to the Mentoris Project whose mission is to support educational initiatives that foster an appreciation of history and culture to encourage and inspire young people to create a stronger future.

Publisher's Cataloging-in-Publication (Provided by Cassidy Cataloguing Services, Inc.)

Names: Barbera, Robert, 1932- author.
Title: How to jump-start your way to real estate wealth / Robert Barbera.
Description: San Marino, CA : The Mentoris Project, [2023]
Identifiers: ISBN: 978-1-947431-54-6 (paperback) | LCCN: 2022949663
Subjects: LCSH: Real estate investment. | Real estate business. | Investments. | Apartment houses. | Wealth. | BISAC: BUSINESS & ECONOMICS / Real Estate / General. | BUSINESS & ECONOMICS / Real Estate / Buying & Selling Homes. | BUSINESS & ECONOMICS / Real Estate / Commercial.
Classification: LCC: HD1382.5 .B37 2023 | DDC: 332.6324--dc23

CONTENTS

Introduction   1

Part One: The Property   5

Chapter One: What Do We Mean by Real Estate Investment?   7
    The Different Types of Real Estate Investments, Pros and Cons   7
        Raw Land   9
        Industrial/Commercial Property   10
        Residential Apartment House   11
    Making Your Decision   11

Chapter Two: Purchasing and Managing Apartment Houses   15
    The Apartment House Business   15
    The Fundamentals   18
        Mind-set   18
        The Owner-Tenant Relationship   22
        Timing the Market   24

Chapter Three: Appraising a Property   27
    The Neighborhood   27
    Street Appeal   29
    Street Appeal Survey   30
    Appraising the Building's Value   33
        Professional Appraising   33
        Comparable Properties   35
        Gross Rent Multiplier   36
        Potential Rent   37
        Net Operating Income   39
        Capitalization Rate   40
        Appreciation   41
        Buyer Beware   41

Reasons I've Walked Away   42
Case Study: Eighty-Eight-Unit Building   44

Chapter Four: Finding Properties   47
Finding a Broker   50
What I Look for in a Building   51

Part Two: Making the Deal   57

Chapter Five: How Much Money Do You Need?   59
Negotiations   59
Escrow   59
Don't Fall in Love   60
Additional Conditions   61
Sticker Shock   62
Example #1: A Four-Unit Apartment House   63
Example #2: A Two-Unit Duplex   65
Depreciation   66
Making a Trade   69
Investment Analysis   71
Internal Rate of Return   72
A Word of Warning   73

Chapter Six: Maximizing Your Capital   77
Raising Capital   77
Other People's Money   79
Don't Touch Your Principal   82
Put Together a Business Plan   84
Ask Questions   86
Debt   87
Minimize Your Down Payment   91
Negotiate the Purchase Price   94
Create a Win-Win   95
Playing Hardball   100
The Psychology of Numbers   102

Stretching Your Dollars   103

Stretching Your Dollars 103
Equity 104
    When Not to Maximize Your Capital 106
    You Are Surrounded by Money 109
Case Study: Management Makes All the Difference 112
Land Value vs. Building Value 115
Insurance 116
Case Study: The Importance of Insurance 117

Chapter Seven: Developing Relationships 119
    Get Your Own House in Order 121
    Contracts 124
When Relationships Change 128
Case Study: The Golden Deal 129

Part Three: Management 135

Chapter Eight: Why Managing Is the Secret Sauce 137
Absentee Landlords 137
Your Team 140
    The Owner 140
    The Manager 141
    Administration 142
    Hiring Professionals 144
Training Your Manager 147
    Personal Appearance and Demeanor 147
    Keep Public Areas Neat and Clean 148
    Public Safety 149
    Apartment Vacancies and Renting 149
    Set Managers Up for Success 151
Preparing to Rent 152
    Discrimination 154
The Psychology of the Owner-Tenant Relationship 155
Finding the Right Tenants 156
Bad Tenants 159
Case Study: The Tenant from Hell 160

Case Study: When Tenants Set up an
    Adversarial Relationship   163
Final Thoughts   167

Appendix: Sample Forms   171
  How to Use the Sample Forms   171
  Vacancy Sign-In Sheet   173
  New Tenant Information   174
  Maintenance Forms   176
    Repair Request   176
    Weekly Summary of Maintenance Requests   176
  Repair Request Form   178
  Weekly Summary of Maintenance Requested by Manager   179
  On-the-Spot Recognition Form   180
  Three (3) Day Notice to Pay Rent or Quit   181
  Thirty (30) Day Notice of Intent to Vacate   182
  Move-Out Form   185
Acknowledgments   188
About the Author   189

INTRODUCTION

The world of real estate investment and apartment management has been very good to me.

I've worked my whole life in jobs ranging from shoeshine boy to window dresser, IRS auditor, credit union exec, restaurant manager, and half a dozen other careers in between and on the side. Married with a family, I always made enough for us to live a secure life. But investing in real estate—and I don't just mean investing money, I mean investing time and energy and focus—was the decision that ultimately built a multimillion-dollar revenue stream. It was real estate ownership and management that created our family's wealth.

I don't come from money. My parents arrived in this country from Italy with a determination to work hard to make a better life for their children. My brother and I started working at a very young age. I was a shoeshine boy at the age of six; for ten cents, I would give you a twenty-minute shoeshine that was a work of art, and I had fun doing it, too. In a couple of years, I had moved on to delivering newspapers. And one day, as I was delivering papers, another newsboy pointed out a man across the street. "That man is rich," the kid told me. "He owns all the apartment buildings on this street." For me, that was all it took. If being rich meant that you owned apartment buildings, someday I was going to own one myself. It's funny how the things we encounter as children set the stage for how we view the world. The money that was in my bank account never made me feel as wealthy as mowing the lawn for my own apartment building did.

But my greatest role model was my mother. Even as I was looking at that man across the street, wealth was being developed right there in my own backyard. My mother had always been interested in real estate. She spent a lifetime parlaying one property into an even bigger one, from a vacant lot all the way up to a sixty-unit apartment complex in Brooklyn. This is particularly impressive because she only had a third-grade education and English was not her first language. From the time I was a kid, she'd have me read the contracts out loud to her and she would memorize the key points. My mother was good with numbers and, boy, she was a tough negotiator. I didn't even realize all the skills I was learning from her; it was an ongoing process, everything from reading those contracts to absorbing how she evaluated, upgraded, and marketed properties. But the most important thing she ever taught me was how much it mattered to have a vision for your future, to always be working toward a dream. Property ownership was always my dream.

Not that I jumped right into real estate. I worked a lot of jobs, eventually realizing I needed a college diploma to get ahead. I spent a couple of years studying on the side before I went to college full-time. In my last year of college, my mother moved out to California and moved in with us. It should go without saying that she bought an apartment house out here (which I'll talk more about later) and that first year, newly graduated from college, I did her taxes. Imagine my surprise when I realized she'd made twice what I'd made in my new job with the IRS. To put it another way, with a college education and a steady salary, I'd made half of what my mother had earned, and she'd only been educated as far as the third grade.

I thought, wow, I am clearly in the wrong business! Right then and there, I started looking into how I could make money from real estate.

You may have had a wake-up call of your own, a moment when you also realized that your daily grind primarily created wealth for other people, and you wanted something better for yourself and for your family. Or maybe you're just starting out and looking to get into real estate on the ground floor (if you'll pardon the pun). Or maybe retirement is on the horizon and you want an investment that will appreciate in value while also keeping you engaged in the world. No matter what stage of life you're in, real estate is worth looking into.

That's what this book is for: helping you figure out where to start.

We'll go over everything—how to evaluate an investment, where to find the money, how to structure deals, and how to look realistically at the problems you may face. While my money was primarily made in residential real estate, there are other ways to invest in real estate. We'll look at the whole picture, pros and cons. With any luck, you may even learn from my mistakes.

I've written some books on finance and building wealth where I suggest you bounce around and read the chapters that are most pertinent to your life. This is not that kind of book. I want you to read it all, read it more than once, think it through, and make a plan about what you'll do when—not if—everything goes wrong (more on that later, but fair warning now that, yes, sometimes the best plans go awry). Positives, such as a steady stream of income and appreciating property values, are balanced by responsibilities: mortgage payments, taxes, finding and retaining good tenants, maintaining clean and attractive properties.

Real estate investment is not for everyone, and that's okay. That's one of the reasons I want to show you the personal side of negotiations and apartment management and all the things that investing in places where people live and work can entail. I want you to see the full picture so you'll have the information you need to decide whether or not real estate investing and management is a good fit for you.

Also, reading this book is no guarantee that you'll have the same success I had. Your mileage may vary. Heck, my mileage varied—not only because of mistakes I made along the way, but because real estate prices go up and down, regulations change, neighborhoods shift. There are a lot of variables you can't control. All the material in this book is predicated on the experiences of the author. Cycles in the real estate economy are unavoidable, and past analysis must always be updated by you doing your own due diligence. Some of the information presented must be understood in its time and context, including the hot and often volatile Southern California real estate market. I will make quite a few disclaimers as we go, but the big one is here: I waive all responsibility for your results. There are too many variables, they are changing constantly, and you have your own tolerance for risk and definition of success. The best I can do with this book—and what I hope I have done—is provide you with a sound understanding of the basic elements needed for success and a look at many of the pitfalls you may encounter with an eye toward helping you to learn from my own mistakes.

I have prospered for fifty years by focusing on real estate and property management, but most of all I have prospered by understanding myself and my own strengths, continually learning by doing, failing, and trying again. If there was any gamble to be made, I always bet on myself, and that, I believe, is the key to my success.

Which brings me to my last point: there is knowing what to do, and then there is actually doing it. I want to help there as well. This isn't going to be just a paint-by-numbers approach; I'm going to show you how important mind-set is to any kind of success, and that includes real estate. I developed a plan for each property that included a backup plan to make sure that if everything went haywire, my family would still be taken care of. That gave me the mental freedom to be able to take needed risks, devote truly insane hours to building my business, and even, when necessary, cut my losses and move on. Furthermore, I guarantee that if you look at being a landlord, say, as a terrible chore or some kind of "How much can I get away with?" game, you will not have the same financial success or—even more important to me—the same joy in life that you will have by taking great care of your tenants and your property. They, not square footage, are your investment in a secure future.

I hope this book helps you along that path.

—Robert Barbera

PART ONE
THE PROPERTY

Chapter One

What Do We Mean by Real Estate Investment?

The Different Types of Real Estate Investments, Pros and Cons

First, let me give you a quick overview of the different types of real estate investments:

You can buy raw land.
You can buy and lease industrial/commercial property.
You can buy and lease residential apartment houses.

I'm going to leave off the table the purchase of single-family homes. You may have one of those, the house you live in, and if so, that's great. For one thing, it's a source of equity you may be able to parlay into an investment property. But buying single-family homes is not, in and of itself, the best investment property you can find.

I figured out early on that the more units you have in a property, the safer your income stream. With a single-family home, if you can't find a tenant for it, your income from the property is zero. That can be a frightening place to be for any length of time, because your expenses don't lessen when there's no one home: you still have to maintain the property, keep up with the mortgage, and pay property taxes. But if that same property were, for instance, a duplex, you would still have some cash coming in from one tenant while you looked for another. The costs for upkeep are roughly the same—it's the same footprint— but that second apartment provides some insurance. Two apartments can also increase your revenue: if, instead of one four-bedroom house, your building offered two two-bedroom apartments, you could rent each apartment for a little over half what you could for the house.

When I started investing in real estate after graduating from college, here's what I was looking at:

- Hard as it is to believe, a two- or three-bedroom house was selling from $12,000 to $15,000 (with an average sticker price of $13,000). The entire house could be rented out at something between $100/month and $150/month. The average was $125/month, which translated to an annual rent of $1,500. The sales price rule of thumb at the time for an income property's value was ten times the annual rent, and that was more or less what I was seeing.

- Apartment houses with two-bedroom units were selling from $9,000 to $10,000 per unit. The average was $8,000/unit, giving a total price for a duplex something around $16,000. The rent ranged from $75/month to $95/month (averaging $85/month), which meant the average annual rent from a (two-unit) duplex was $85 x 12 months x 2 units, or $2,040/year. This was close to a sales price of eight times the annual gross rent.

What I realized was that the down payment and mortgage payments would have been roughly the same for both properties. If I lived in one unit of the apartment house, the tenant of the other unit would pay rent, which in turn would cover a lot of the expenses. Furthermore, the overall maintenance on the property would be the same whether I owned a residential house or two two-bedroom units.

Owning a second unit with a tenant is a great way to cut expenses and, at the same time, start accumulating equity and savings that can then be parlayed into bigger and better properties. But by the same logic, owning an apartment complex with three or four units (or more) would be even better. The analysis looked so great, I couldn't resist it. I kept looking until I found an eight-unit apartment house and I went for it, using negotiation and leverage to make a deal that was a stretch for us at the time, but became the foundation of our financial future.

Inflation has distorted these figures from my past, but the relative costs and opportunities between a residential house and an apartment house purchase remain roughly the same. The numbers look absurd to us now, but $15,000 was a fortune back then; I remember trying to raise the rent from $72.50/month to $75 and facing some extremely angry tenants. These days, that's not even your water bill! The important point is that, relatively speaking, everything has moved in tandem. Do the analysis for yourself with the numbers in front of you and see what makes the most sense for your financial future.

One caveat about the "more units is better" idea: this is also the philosophy that leads to cramming as many human beings into each square foot as possible, and that is a lousy way to do business. I'll talk more about that when I discuss appraising apartment houses a little later on. So don't go crazy trying to carve out units from walk-in closets. Rather, it's useful for you to think about how you can invest in a property that maximizes your investment while minimizing risk, *and* one that provides an excellent living space for your residents. While single-family homes may do the latter (and they don't always—I'm sure we've all viewed some single-family properties that were dark, poorly built, and barely maintained), I don't think single-family homes are an ideal investment. Take it with a grain of salt if you like, but I can only give you my best advice.

Raw Land

Buying raw land constitutes the least amount of work for the owner. Other than the purchase price and ensuing mortgage, there is little to no expense for upkeep beyond the property taxes, which tend to be small for unimproved land. As a long-term investment, owning raw land can be very rewarding if the location pops. That's the upside. The downside is that the location may never pop. It may still appreciate over time; I would expect it to at least keep up with inflation. But raw land is not an income-producing investment. It's more like hanging onto a painting in the attic with the hopes that someday enough other people will start liking the artist; in other words, it's a bit of a gamble. Now, I suggest that real estate is still preferable to a painting in the attic because, while artistic taste is fickle, people will always need land to build on. But you must take into account that some areas may not be ripe for development for a long, long time.

Industrial/Commercial Property

The good news is that industrial and commercial properties typically have very long leases, and major corporations pay their rent on time. In addition, there's something called "triple net leases," which translate to no maintenance on your end, making your life much easier. You're also a businessperson dealing with another business; it's all the language of contracts, so there isn't as much room for interpersonal conflict. Also, you know the old real estate adage that the three most important things are "location, location, location"? With industrial property, sometimes locations that are less desirable for residential areas are exactly what they're looking for.

Commercial properties, mind you, need an excellent location even more than residential apartments—although their definition of "excellent" may vary. While apartment residents might want quiet, commercial tenants want a lot of traffic, ideally foot traffic. Again, long leases give your cash flow stability. The downsides to both commercial and industrial properties, however, are the same: they generally require large down payments and they can be slow to re-rent. You should look at how long any of the properties have remained without a commercial or industrial tenant and then try to figure out why. That can provide you with good information. Some things may be within your control to improve or prevent, but other things, including an inaccessible or otherwise difficult location, might be insurmountable.

Residential Apartment House

The advantages to owning a residential apartment are many. In fact, this entire book is about how you can make money by investing in and managing apartment houses. Here are some of the pros.

First, the down payment requirements are limited compared to that of commercial/retail/industrial properties. Second, people will always need a place to live. Given the right property, your apartment units will always be in demand. Apartments are typically easier to rent, and you have more of them. This is important. Multiple apartments can provide quicker cash flow from multiple tenants; even if you lose a resident, you still have income from other apartment units to tide you over until you can re-rent. None of that is necessarily true with commercial, retail, or industrial properties.

Residential apartments do, however, come with some disadvantages: they require ongoing upkeep and developing good relationships with your residents. Good management is the secret sauce to making money in residential properties. A failure to recognize that this is not a one-time or purely monetary purchase, but instead one that requires ongoing investment of both time and money, can prove fatal.

Making Your Decision

There is no one right answer in real estate investment. The only wrong answer is to kid yourself about your own capabilities and (even more important) your willingness to become involved in one investment or the other. If you are ever going to be brutally honest with yourself, the time to do it is now—before you invest your heart and soul, not to mention your life's savings, into real estate. If you don't like people, owning and managing an apartment complex is probably not the right move for you. Raw land requires far less work on an ongoing basis, but while the land will likely appreciate over the long term, it may never "pop," and your money would have appreciated more in some other vehicle, such as stocks or a business venture. There are always both risks and an opportunity cost to consider.

In fact, let's consider that now. You have a certain amount of money to invest, and you are perhaps wondering if you should put it in a stock portfolio or put it in real estate. That is a great thing to think about! And I can't tell you the right answer. At the moment you read this, stocks may be in a correction, and perhaps more attractive (remember, you want to buy low and sell high—although that's the only stock advice I feel comfortable giving you!). Or the stock market might be wildly overvalued, or worse, there might be a bubble about to burst. The same can be true in real estate.

Here's the difference: the stock market is reported on hour by hour; some people may even be glued to it minute by minute during particularly volatile times. The media constantly reports and/or speculates on market valuations. With real estate, that doesn't happen. Real estate values are reported sporadically, they vary wildly depending on location, and you certainly won't see ups and downs in the news on a daily (much less hourly) basis. And yet, real estate infrastructure is enormous, a giant owned by millions of people, and its total worth is believed to far outweigh stock values. For many people, their greatest single asset is their home. And while there have been corrections in the real estate market, the trajectory tilts upward in most areas.

In addition to worrying about returns, however, many people are concerned about liquidity. Yes, stocks are generally more liquid than real estate in that you can always sell them—but it doesn't mean you can always sell them at a profit. A market dip at the wrong time and selling can wipe out years' worth of investment. I don't even want to talk about margin accounts! With real estate, if you find yourself needing liquidity, equity loans are often available. You are not liquidating your asset with a loan the way you do when you sell stock, although you are borrowing against it. Consider your own tolerance for risk and ability to rebound after a setback.

For me, the thing I've always liked about real estate is that it is tangible. Although I do now have a stock portfolio, for a long time I didn't. I had dabbled in the market as a very young man. It was tremendously exciting and volatile, and ultimately I got burned. I no longer "play" the market; instead, I use it to invest in companies I believe in. I think the stock market is a great way to own a piece of American business, and I'm not going to discourage you from looking into it. But for me, well, I just can't fall in love with a stock certificate the way I fall in love with an apartment house. It's real; it's something I can improve upon and directly help to make it thrive.

Diversity in your investments is always going to be the right answer. Take advantage of what each investment can do for you. The purpose of this book is not to debate whether or not you should put your money in the stock market, in real estate, or in your mattress. My goal here is to give you the inside scoop of what it's like to invest in and manage apartment houses.

Let's get to it.

CHAPTER TWO

PURCHASING AND MANAGING APARTMENT HOUSES

The Apartment House Business

The business of renting and managing apartment houses is considered by the Internal Revenue Service as a passive activity—although, as you will see, there is little about it that is truly passive. According to the National Apartment Association, 39 million Americans—almost 1 in 8—currently live in apartments. The U.S. Department of Housing and Urban Development said in 2017 that there would be a need for 4.6 million new apartment homes by 2030 to meet increased demand; we're five years in as I write these words and I doubt if we're close to meeting that mark.

Many things are driving the desire for apartments, but one is older people, who may want a downsized lifestyle without the need to maintain their own home (or do yard work; even I don't do that anymore, and I used to take care of my properties as well as my own house). Another factor is young people who are getting married and starting families later, and so they're renting longer. A growing population also means a greater need for housing, and a growing urban population means a lot of that housing is going to have to be apartments, where you can build up, not just out. Whatever the circumstances that are influencing this growth, you will start to recognize a refrain running through this book, which is that people will always need a place to live, and apartment house ownership is one way for you to be part of that solution.

There are tremendous challenges for providing land for development and quality construction; development requires huge investments of both money and time, which can put you in a bind. You need to make sure you have sufficient resources to withstand the time it takes to get permits, complete construction, and attract tenants. Delays in any of these steps can put an incredible strain on your cash flow, as you will continue to have money going out in terms of mortgage payments and construction costs, without any cash flow coming in from leasing the units. If this is the route you want to go, you may need partners and you will definitely need a business plan that includes a buffer for every possible obstacle. You would also be well served by finding mentors who have done this, ideally ones who have both succeeded and failed. It is imperative to learn from other people's mistakes and not just their stories of glory. Those may be fun to hear and even more fun to tell, but the lessons that will keep you from losing your shirt are learned from listening to the obstacles they faced and how they handled them, for better and for worse.

The purchase of an existing complex provides its own set of challenges. In Southern California, for instance, complexes built before current earthquake codes needed to be retrofitted for safety, often at tremendous cost. Perhaps more subtly, some existing complexes were built for greed rather than for creating a space people would want to live in. Over one hundred years ago, New York City enacted a law requiring windows in every apartment, but developers often got around the law by including "interior" windows—in other words, from one room to another—or even worse, slits that looked out (as much as you could look out through a slit in the wall) on a central air shaft. While those days are behind us, it's still critical for each apartment to provide sufficient light and air to the tenant. The one thing you never want is to be someone's last resort; that will not attract the kind of tenants who will anchor your financial stability.

Apartment housing ownership requires developing good relationships, a theme I will return to again and again. You don't just need relationships with contractors you trust, and with bankers who trust you; you also need to develop a sense of mutual respect with government regulators, real estate agents, maintenance staff and other employees, and most of all, with your tenants. The days of pitting the greedy landlord against the penniless widow are long behind us, and I hope that particular stereotype is quickly lost to history. On the contrary, I believe that individual owners are the key to quality housing because they alone have a personal stake in each property and really each individual unit. With government housing, for instance, there's no individual owner who is themselves directly impacted by a complex falling into ruin. Without individual responsibility and connection, even the best of intentions can't keep pace with the reality of upkeep, shifting neighborhoods, managing employees and contract maintenance workers, and the thousand other little details that make a difference between a place that houses people and a place that merely warehouses them.

This is true for individuals as well as for governments; you never want to have so many units that you can no longer visit them all. I stopped at just over five hundred units. This was a plan I had put into place when I was at roughly one hundred units. I did the math and figured out that five hundred units would keep everyone in the organization (gardeners, management, painters, bookkeepers) fully employed, providing maximum bang for the buck, if you will. Over the years, I was constantly "upgrading" my properties, not just to have more and better units, but also so that they would be closer to each other. I got rid of outliers that required half a day to go visit. I wanted things to be easy and efficient, and at the same time, personal. Devolving into a faceless corporation is not the end goal. Like government housing, that, too, can lead to a weakening of the relationships that make a difference in people's lives and ultimately in your success.

In other words, I believe that both renters and owners are best served by private apartment complex ownership. Fitting people into dark cubicles without personal responsibility (on your side or on theirs) ignores their humanity, to everyone's detriment. Apartment houses succeed when an invested owner and a resident both have a stake in their relationship. They can both take pride in their involvement. Our society is elevated from feudal lords and serfs to a legal-minded people who are interdependent by choice. There is an awareness to our relationships, a mutual benefit. Rather than defined as the rich and the poor, the lord and the serf, we are instead both equal human beings, one who has shelter to provide and the other with a need for that shelter. As with any product, if you provide substandard service, you will lose good tenants to people who provide a better service. Notice I don't say a "cheaper" service. More on that later, but no, I don't believe that a race to the bottom serves anyone. Ownership of apartment houses is not a get-rich-quick scheme by any means. Rather, it takes years of paying down debt, maintaining care, and investing time, sweat, and tears before you see the rewards. It is meant to be a fair exchange of value: the owner is building equity while the resident finds an apartment to be the most practical way to budget their housing.

Ultimately, the owner must persevere, creating value to attract tenants while at the same time building relationships, working with quality vendors, dealing with government oversight, and maintaining upkeep on the property inside and out. It is not a short-term plan, and it is definitely not for the faint of heart. But people will always need a place to live, and the rewards for doing so are both tangible and ineffably heart-warming.

The Fundamentals

Mind-set

Before we talk about acquiring a property, let me tell you about an even more fundamental step, and that is adjusting your mind-set. You may know intellectually that acquiring property—whether it be land for development or units to lease, either commercial or residential—is going to tie up a lot of your resources, but I guarantee you have not sat down and adequately thought through what that is going to mean for your life for the next several years. So let us take a moment for some honest talk.

Buying property is a major, life-altering choice. It will demand financial resources beyond what you imagine, it will devour your time, and it will likely alter many of your relationships. Let's take each in turn.

First, financial resources. In other words, your money. I expect that you will put together a business plan before you make an offer, but it's likely that the first plan will be a little too rosy. That's a good place to start—you want to believe it's possible, after all, or you wouldn't even try—but you should also make a second plan, one for your eyes only. I want you to assume that everything goes wrong. For instance, new owners are responsible for any code violations, even if those violations occurred under the previous owner. I bought a building once, and no inspection reports were included in the deal. Were they hidden from me on purpose or simply out of negligence? Who can say? But I ended up having to pay for half a dozen minor code violations that I didn't know were there. Another time, I was arrested—actually arrested and thrown in jail overnight—to make sure I would appear in court the following day for a code violation that existed before I bought the property and for which I had not received any written communication; the notices had all gone to the previous owner, who had not passed them along.

I'm not saying you should plan to end up in jail, but you do want to set aside funds to fix whatever may be broken. Prepare for the worst—and I mean the absolute worst. What if you die? How is your family protected? Obviously, I don't wish that on you, but I do wish you would buy sufficient insurance to cover the possibility. You don't want your family to lose their house, for instance, if you die and suddenly all this debt you acquired along with the property is now on their doorstep.

Talk to people who have already purchased property and learn from their stories as I hope you'll learn from mine. Talk to insurance agents (and don't just assume they're angling for a commission). Talk to your lawyer, to your bank. Learn as much as you can about all the possibilities, not just the sunshine and flowers of success stories. Gobble up information and try to get it from as many sources as possible. Ask people who have done it what they wish they'd known early in their career. Brainstorm with a friend or a partner all the things that could go wrong, including but not limited to fraud, natural disasters, a burst pipe, or a sudden change in regulations or interest rates.

Imagine that your entire stake is lost; what would you do? There is tremendous value in imagining the worst, not to wallow in it, but to see that, yes, there is always a way out. With my first eight-unit apartment building, I knew that if everything went to hell, I could always sell our house and have our family move into one of the units. Was this my first choice? No. Was it nonetheless a way to make sure my family had a roof over their heads while we got back on our financial feet? Yes. Having a backup plan for when things go wrong is what gives you the necessary courage to take the risk, and then of course you work your butt off to make sure you don't need to default to Plan B.

One nonnegotiable is to budget for the insurance policies. If everything goes smoothly, that doesn't mean insurance was a mistake, it just means you were lucky this time, and I'm happy for you. Insurance is the one expense you hope you never make back. You should also include some padding to cover the unexpected. Things will happen that you can't specifically have predicted or prevented, but you can predict that *something* will go wrong. It is your responsibility to make sure the entire project doesn't go belly-up for want of a nail. That is what stepping into ownership means.

This is what I want you to get your head around. You are not gambling—you are making the best possible choices for the long-term success of your project. It is a different headspace than you're probably used to, especially if you've been someone else's employee up until now. You have to be willing to see the bad news and make the hard choices with everyone's well-being in mind. Once you've taken that on, you've really taken your first step toward success.

So that's money. Next is time. I know you realize that property ownership and management is an investment, but just as it's going to take more money than you expect, it's also going to take more time. A lot more time.

I bought our first apartment building while I still worked for the IRS. In other words, I had a day job. Weekends were spent going over to the building and maintaining the property. I mowed the lawn myself. The family was involved in cleaning and painting empty units to make them attractive to new tenants. My wife kept the books in the evenings, after dinner. We lived and breathed that building, and the next one, and the next, until finally it became more than we could do as a family, and I had enough of a cash flow to start hiring help to do the maintenance. It was important to me to create my own management company so that everything was ultimately our responsibility; again, no faceless corporation managing things. Each of my kids, upon coming of age, had to manage one of the properties—to learn the ropes and to learn to care. I want you to recognize that it's not just something where you commit the funds and sign the papers and collect the checks. Property management is a full-time second job for the next five to twenty years.

Are you willing to make that commitment? If the answer is no, it's best to figure that out before you've poured your life's savings into a property, not after. I've had a lot of friends who tried their hand at buying a rental property only to discover it was much harder than they thought it would be. Maybe they came into it a little too naive. Maybe they thought, "Hey, if Robert can do it, so can I!" Which, actually, I believe to be true—if I can do it, so can you. That's why I'm writing this book! But don't kid yourself that I didn't work very, very hard, and that you won't have to work hard as well.

Finally, let's talk about relationships. I've already mentioned how buying property is going to have an impact on your wallet and your free time. Do you really think those things won't also have an impact on your relationships? This is one of the reasons it's critical to have that Plan B in place. Fighting over money is really fighting over feelings of safety, and it can be fatal to your marriage. Your significant other and your children have to be protected by insurance if something happens to you, and by having a solid Plan B if something happens to everything except you. Your ambitions are noble, but you can't reach them at the expense of your kids living out of your car. Being brutally pessimistic in your expectations will serve you well, because it will force you to make sure you have a way to take care of those you love even if things go wrong. This, in turn, will allow them to relax and allow you to show up as the best possible version of yourself with them, because no one—not you, not them—is in panic or survival mode.

Once that's taken care of, however, you still have extended family and friends to handle. I'm not going to lie; not all of your relationships will survive this new you. For one thing, you're not going to have disposable cash and time to hang out with people or take large family vacations the way you may have in the past. You're going to be working two jobs (more on not giving up your day job later), you're going to be obsessed with this new investment and making it all work out, and you're going to be tired. Some of your friends will fall away naturally when you don't have time for them, and that's okay. Others will become jealous of what you're building or turn into naysayers out of fear or envy, and that, my friend, is much more difficult to navigate.

When I say you need to be willing to listen to the worst that can happen, I mean from people who have gone through it and survived, not from the bozo on the next barstool. You have to recognize that your success might be intimidating to some people and simply not listen to them. You are making difficult decisions from a place of (I sincerely hope) knowledge and forethought. If your best friend suddenly calls you selfish for skipping happy hour to catch up on the books or some much-needed rest, it might be time to take a break from that relationship. This probably isn't something you planned for in your profit and loss projections, but it's your life, and if you want to put the hard work into property ownership, then I, for one, believe that you will be amply rewarded.

The Owner-Tenant Relationship

The apartment house industry is constantly changing. Let me give you an example. A friend of mine had a resident who had been leasing a condominium from him for almost forty-five years. Back then, when you rented a condo, the condition was virtually bare. The new tenant would expect to paint the place, put up their own drapes, lay down their own rugs, and make the condominium their long-term residence. My friend's agreement with his tenant (a widow with two children) was typical for the day: there was no credit report, and their agreement was verbal. He was not a hands-on landlord and she or someone in her family fixed anything that might be broken. As needed, he hired experts to do such things as upgrade the plumbing or replace a water-damaged wall. She settled in and made the condominium her home; in fact, when my friend's health was failing and he was settling his affairs, he decided to sell the condominium to her. As far as I know, she lives there still.

Very little of this would play out the same way today. First of all, written rental agreements are critical, and I don't advocate you ever doing business without one—even if you're renting to a family member. In fact, especially then! It's important that legal agreements are in writing so that everyone has the same understanding of your agreement. Security deposits are now required, and in exchange, the resident has an expectation of such things as freshly painted walls, clean apartments, window and floor coverings, appliances, lighting fixtures, air-conditioning . . . the list goes on. When things go wrong, the tenant just picks up the phone and it is the owner's responsibility to provide what's missing or fix what's broken. Adequate parking, play areas, well-lit entryways, and other amenities outside the apartment itself are also important. Government regulations are constantly changing to incorporate safety upgrades, lighting, zoning, size of units, parking requirements, potential discrimination, control of rental rates, required notices of hazards such as asbestos, water quality, eviction, and the handling of problems with undesirable renters.

People also have a lot of different reasons for renting as well. They may rent because it's more affordable than home ownership, or because they have no time or interest to maintain a home themselves. They may be busy professionals or they may travel a lot, or they may be college students wanting to live near, but not on, campus. Apartment rental is the right choice for some people based on affordability, living style, family makeup, professional obligations, a more transient moment of their lives (such as college), or simply that they don't want the responsibility of owning their own home.

Just as there is no particular common background or classification for residents, so, too, are owners more and more varied. They can range from a blue-collar worker trying to create supplemental income or save for retirement all the way to a professional investor using property as a means of long-term investment, and everything in between. The concept of landlord-and-tenant is an old one, and the nomenclature is rarely used today except in legal documents, to keep it consistent with existing laws and precedents. Today the relationship is thought of as owner-and-resident instead. One provides a commodity that the other needs. The apartment house owner is a business owner—that's really the mind-set you need. You are not dabbling or "renting out a room"; you are building a business. You maximize your bottom line by understanding what you provide to the resident: peace and quiet, adequate living facilities, a sense of home. Remember that the resident's rent check represents a significant proportion of their budget, and they have every right to expect value for the cost. Just as you won't get far selling pens that don't write, you won't build a business by offering apartments that don't meet a resident's needs.

Times change, vocabulary changes, but one thing I want to point out that existed way back between my friend and his tenant still remains true today: the benefits of a mutually respectful relationship. Each of them, owner and resident, respected the other's position. Both took pride in the unit; one the pride of ownership, the other the pride of caring for their home. It was this relationship that benefited both of them for almost half a century, and it will benefit you as well.

Timing the Market

Let me tell you why I think apartment houses will remain a good investment. First of all, demand exceeds supply. As our population increases, more people need places to live. Certain communities, especially in or near urban areas, are seeing an even greater uptick as more people choose to live there. Remember those 4.6 million new apartment units that the U.S. is going to need by 2030? New York, Dallas-Fort Worth, and Houston alone will need about a quarter of a million units each. Real estate values are going up, construction costs are rising, and the value of home ownership has, in the last few years, gone through the roof. (Note that these are often cyclical, but they are true at the time I write this.) All of these things mean that if you own an apartment building, you are in a position to see your rent income increase as well as the equity in your property, giving you more resale value (not to mention equity to leverage) down the line.

If you do not yet own an apartment complex, however, these same circumstances may make it look as if you've missed the boat.

I won't deny that there are overpriced properties on the market, but there are also still opportunities to be had. I know so many investors who waited on the sidelines to purchase an apartment house only to regret their inaction later.

I believe one of the biggest mistakes you can make is waiting for the "right time" to buy and never actually doing it. Why? Because this is not a short-term game. You are not trying to "flip" an apartment complex. You are in this for the long haul. And over the long term, property values have traditionally increased beyond inflation. If you miss the bottom or pay "too much" in the moment, it doesn't really matter in the long run. The apartment house, unlike your own home, generates income as you go along. Part of that income is invested back into the complex, part of it goes toward paying the mortgage, and part of it goes to you, ideally for you to parlay into yet more property. By the time you're ready to sell it, if that day ever comes, the price you paid for it will be largely irrelevant.

CHAPTER THREE

APPRAISING A PROPERTY

The Neighborhood

To understand a property's potential value as an apartment complex, the first thing you need to do, before you even visit the property itself, is visit the neighborhood.

When it comes to real estate, the top three concerns really are "location, location, location."

I always walk the neighborhood. I'm looking for places where I feel comfortable. I like to be around people who are friendly. When I look at a neighborhood, I'm always thinking, "Would I want to live here? Are these people I'd feel comfortable sitting down for coffee with?" It really has nothing to do with their income and everything to do with "Are they nice?" I have a friend who owned an apartment house in a very prosperous neighborhood. He made good money because the rents were high; he had some pretty wealthy tenants. And let me tell you, the stories he had! The people who lived in his building made his life miserable, always complaining about this or feeling entitled to that. I'm not saying that's true of all wealthy people, but it sure was true of his tenants.

Me, I didn't want that kind of hassle. There will always be problems, but sometimes you can pick the kinds of problems you want to deal with. There was another neighborhood I visited, not nearly as wealthy, and that didn't work for me either because everyone I met with was mean. I don't care about your politics or your bank balance—I just want you to be polite! Now, for you, that might not be such a big deal. You might want the energy that comes from this kind of neighborhood or the potential growth that comes from that one, or the bigger rents that come from that other neighborhood over there . . . that's great. Again, pick your problems. But for me, I tried to cultivate nice people and avoid the not-nice ones. That's the first thing I look for in a neighborhood.

At the same time, I'm a businessman. I'm also trying to find any hidden problems. For instance, as I walk around, I'm checking to see if there are a lot of "For Rent" signs on the block. If every building has vacancies, what's going on there? What do they know that I don't know?

Neighborhoods are never static. They are always in transition, either becoming more desirable or less so with every passing day. Obviously, as with stocks, you want to buy something that is undervalued and going to increase in desirability. Unfortunately, cycles are always in flux and it's not always easy to make that assessment.

But there are some clues. Walk the neighborhood. How safe do you feel? Are broken windows allowed to stay broken, or do problems get repaired, painted over, spruced up? Is it overcrowded? Is there excessive noise? What's the crime rate—petty crime and theft are good markers, but if there's gang warfare going on, you definitely want to know about that as well. What are the schools like? Is the public transportation adequate or even existent? What are the city services? Is there good infrastructure and upkeep of roads, rubbish, streetlights? You need to dig into the local codes as well. Red flags include a hodgepodge of codes and restrictive burdens on businesses and homeowners; even if they won't affect you directly, they will have an impact on how the community can grow. I probably don't have to tell you to stay away from places that are heading from general neighborhood neglect into the maws of actual blight.

Positive signs, on the other hand, include parks, community services, upscale shopping districts, professional office buildings, libraries, museums, theaters, adequate parking facilities, and access to main thoroughfares. Digging deeper, you want to find uniform zoning codes and competent services such as fire departments, police, and city officials. Ideally, you are looking for neighborhoods that are trending up. Keep your ear to the ground for announcements of new facilities, from improved public transportation to malls to entertainment districts.

Areas tend to attract certain socioeconomic levels. This doesn't mean you only want to rent to young, urban professionals; everyone needs a safe and attractive place to live. But it is important for you to understand people's characteristics in the location in which you are investing quite an enormous amount of money, time, and energy. It will help everyone if you understand them and their needs and are in a position to meet those needs. Studio apartments that might be ideal for a transient population such as graduate students or young professionals who travel constantly for work will not provide a great experience for families with young children. Meanwhile, an outdoor play area for small kids would not be a draw for, say, college students. You must also understand the community because so much of your success depends on connecting with your residents. You need to have mutual respect and open lines of communication so that whatever differences you do have don't interfere with your relationship.

Street Appeal

While you're looking at neighborhoods, I also want you to be looking at buildings. Not ones you are interested in buying—let's not have you falling in love with any place just yet. Instead, I want you to get your feet wet in a very general way by visiting several properties that were sold some time ago, so there's no pressure. I want you to compare the apartment houses and neighborhoods by using a simple Street Appeal Survey:

STREET APPEAL SURVEY

__ Neighborhood upkeep

__ Trash

__ Graffiti

__ Streetlights

__ How safe do you feel on the street during the day?

__ How safe do you feel on the street at night?

__ Overall crime rate

__ Violent crime rate

__ Adequate parking

__ Public transportation

__ Variety of shops

__ Bars

__ Restaurants

__ Grocery stores

__ Schools:

    __ Convenient location

    __ Quality

__ Income level

__ Office buildings

__ Gas stations

__ Other apartment complexes

__ Noise level

__ Parks

__ Libraries

__ Fire department

__ Theaters/museums/cultural anchors

Go ahead and give a simple letter grade of A through F for each question. Don't overthink it. When you're done, you'll probably be able to tell at a glance if you would have invested in this neighborhood or not; we're all pretty well trained to understand the difference between a B and a D, much less an A and an F. If you want, you can give each property a number score by translating the letters to numbers: A is 4,

B is 3, C is 2, D is 1, and F is 0. Again, we've all spent our childhoods understanding the nuances of the GPA.

Next, get a little nosy. Check out the inside of the apartment complex. Is there a vacancy? Take a tour. Introduce yourself to a resident and ask them some questions about their experience with the building and the management team. If you see service people, stop and talk to them. You may meet a manager willing to talk about their experiences with the property and the residents. Ask neighbors some questions. Use your own judgment as well: is this a place you would like to live, and if so, what appeals to you? Would it have been right for you at a different stage of your life? What would you not have appreciated? What do you find off-putting now?

I have you look at the neighborhood first because an apartment house doesn't exist in a vacuum. If you love hanging out at a neighborhood bar with friends and being able to walk home, is that possible in this location? Is the neighborhood professional or working class? Does it feel overcrowded? Isolated? Is there a church nearby, or a temple within walking distance, or a park with a playground? What does this neighborhood have to support some people and what is it missing for others?

Keep notes of what you liked and what you didn't, as well as anything other people felt strongly about (the good and the bad). We'll talk more about what specifically to look for inside the building a little later. This is to get you to start paying attention to the big picture, and also to what makes a difference for people. Not just what makes a resident decide to rent, but what keeps them in their unit.

You will always—always—find a mix of good and bad. For instance, you might find that there's good public transportation, but the bus stops right in front of the complex and riders routinely leave garbage around the bench at the bus stop. Maybe there's no manager available at the location, but on the other hand you find that the residents stick around for the long term, with very little turnover. The entryway may be dirty and the paint may be peeling, but the building itself has a well-used footprint on a small lot, or perhaps separate entrances for the units, providing plenty of privacy. A college within walking distance might mean a steady supply of undergraduates looking to live off-campus, but that might be balanced by noisy parties. A high crime rate could exist at the same time that a new mall was going up. Sometimes there's a correlation; other times it's just a mix of good and bad, positive and negative, or even things that are positive to some and negative to others. The important thing is for you to start seeing things you never noticed before and take into account variables you might never have considered.

I highly recommend you go on some of these visits with a friend or a partner and talk it out afterward. You will each have noticed different things, and you will care about different things. We are all different and we all bring different strengths and opinions to the table. And because of that, we can help each other expand our understanding of the world.

Once you've visited half a dozen or so, start comparing the properties. The first thing that will stand out is that no property is perfect. This is good to learn early! Some properties will have problems that you, as the owner, can do something about. Others will have problems that are insurmountable. I once looked at a building that had a unit in the center that had no windows. No windows! Who was I supposed to rent that to? No one likes to live like veal. Similarly, I turned down a property where none of the bathrooms had windows, only vents. Someone else might have thought that was no big deal—obviously, someone had built it that way, so it flew under someone's radar. But for me, it gave every unit an unpleasant element that I didn't feel comfortable passing along to my tenants.

Other differences between the properties will help you to see what really matters to the people you want to serve and what doesn't. This will all help train your eye and your expertise. I also want you to look at the prices: the purchase price, how much the units are renting for, the value of the property itself. You may be surprised. Look at every property with an eye toward whether or not you would want to live there. Thinking like a resident is a terrific strategy. Do you feel you would be getting value for your money? If you would not find it acceptable to live in a particular apartment house, I would vote against you buying it. Sure, there are lots of ways for the owner to improve things, but there are also lots of things that are not within your control. Hold out for a place that's a better fit for you.

All of this will help you train yourself on what to pay attention to when you are ready to buy. When you are at that stage, I highly recommend that your first visit to a neighborhood be on your own. Do your own analysis before you go out with a charismatic broker or seller, or someone else with their own agenda and the ability to influence you. The more you do this, the better you'll get, and the more you will see what a minimum score would have to be for you to be willing to put your money into a location.

Appraising the Building's Value

Professional Appraising

You will learn how to appraise over time, but no one will expect you to be an expert your first time in the room. That doesn't mean you should set yourself up to be taken advantage of. Ideally, you will know other people who have bought and sold apartment houses and you can ask them questions and learn from their mistakes, as I hope you will learn from mine in this book. Get out there and network! You will make friends with people who have the same interests you do, you might find a mentor or two, you may even end up meeting potential business partners down the line. At the very least, you will learn by hearing other people talk shop. And while you are educating yourself by reading, meeting, and talking, there are also professionals whose expertise you can hire.

First, there are real estate brokers. Real estate brokers are just what they sound like: professionals who broker deals between a seller and a potential buyer. Just like real estate agents when you're looking to buy your own house or condo. Listing brokers pretty much all use the same formula to calculate value, although the seller's broker is of course trying to make sure the seller gets the best possible price, and the buyer's broker is instead looking out for the interest of their client.

That said, both brokers are invested in the deal being made: if there's no deal, there's no commission. Eventually, a price comes together.

You can also hire appraisers who work for a fee. There is a whole field of professionals who have an education and vast experience understanding the construction of a property; how well it was built; whether or not there's deferred maintenance; the ages and conditions of the plumbing, the walls, the electricity, the doors . . . it's exhaustive. And it's not just the physical building: they also research public ownership, zoning laws, neighborhood demographics. The neighborhood has an intrinsic value. How far is it to the nearest market? What are the schools like? The list goes on and on.

Just like I had you do in that neighborhood survey, these professionals will then grade the property. And here's something you may not know: apartment houses only have to rate a C. Average is just fine in residential properties, as opposed to, say, a hospital, which for obvious reasons has to be an A.

You may have an appraiser, but you're not the only one. The banks have their own professional appraisers because they're putting even more into the property than you are, at least to start. Everyone wants answers to the same questions: what's the quality of the construction, how's the roof, is the sewer system bedeviled by roots, how far is the fire hydrant, how's the sanitation? You are not going to know the answers to this just by taking a tour. Professionals will be used, and their reports are required reading. This is how you learn what to look for—and how you figure out whether or not a building is worth your investment.

There are so many variables that make each property unique, it can sometimes feel not just that you're comparing apples to oranges, but to watermelons or yaks. And yet, at the core, you need to evaluate each apartment house against reasonably comparable units with an eye toward expected returns on your investment. Would people pay enough money to live in these units to make it worth buying? However you go about it, that is the question that needs to be answered.

The more properties you review before buying, the less likely you are to make an impulsive, and often regrettable, decision. There are several different ways for you to get a ballpark estimate of what an income property is worth.

Comparable Properties

Start by looking at comparable properties. Don't forget that, just like when you are buying a single-family home, the asking price is just the starting point. It is not set in stone. What's important is for you to have some way to evaluate whether or not the asking price makes sense. How you do that is to look at other properties similar in size and neighborhood that are either currently for sale or were recently sold. You will probably notice a wide range of prices.

There are many reasons why a particular property's price will vary from the overall market. The asking price may be high because there's an expectation that property values will rise for many reasons, such as a hot real estate market, neighborhood improvements, or the announcement of a major employer coming to the area. Sometimes, however, the owners are just testing the waters to see if someone is eager enough to buy it at any price. I don't recommend that you be that someone.

A low price, on the other hand, may reflect inherent problems such as deferred maintenance or code violations. It could also mean the owners are looking for a quick sale because of cash flow problems or personal emergencies, death, or divorce. You can't always figure out the reasons, but it's always worth a try. Sometimes you can get a real bargain because people are looking to sell for personal reasons; all they want is to be rid of a property (I've been in that position myself; I'll tell you that story a little later), so it's a win-win—you take the property off their hands for a price that works for both of you.

Other times, the personal element can be a disaster. Sometimes, for instance, you can be working with heirs to a property who themselves may have an inflated sense of what their inheritance should be. They may also be fighting among themselves, and if they are all equal owners, they all need to agree for the sale to go through. Their personal family drama may play out with you as a minor character; this is not a good place to be. Some deals just can't be made, especially where there is personal rivalry involved, and you may just have to walk away. Finding out the reason for the sale can give you insight into the dynamics at play so you can have a better shot at knowing when to negotiate and when to walk away.

Gross Rent Multiplier

Having an appraiser or a broker on your side, as well as looking at a lot—a lot!—of comparable properties before you settle on one, can help you figure out a ballpark valuation for a property. But there's another tool you can use to give you a quick estimate, and that is the GRM, or gross rent multiplier.

Here's how it works: You add up the annual rent for each unit and then you multiply it by some number, usually between 7 and 15. That gives you a sense of what the property is worth. So, for instance, a building has four units. Each unit is rented out for $1,000/month, so $12,000/year each, so that's $48,000 total in actual rent. Multiply that by a GRM of 10 and you get a valuation of $480,000 for the building. Simple, right?

Of course, it's not quite that straightforward. First of all, I can hear you saying to me, "Robert, where did you get the GRM of 10?" And that is a great question.

When I first started out, the GRM was 8, more or less across the board. The number gives you a sense of how long it will take to recoup your investment. Remember, this method doesn't take into account how much you'll be putting into the property in terms of insurance, overhead, mortgage interest, and taxes, so don't be fooled into thinking a GRM of 8 means you're free and clear in eight years. But generally speaking, the lower the GRM, the sooner you will start to see a return on your investment.

Now, I've been in this business for 50 years. GRMs started creeping up from 8 to 9 and then to 10 (which was pretty much my limit; I'm not sure I ever went beyond that), and now I've seen them all the way up to 15. This is, to me, an overvaluation of a property, but people can get away with it because both rents and property values have skyrocketed in recent years. So how do you figure out what a reasonable GRM should be?

Work backwards. See what other, comparable properties are selling for and figure out their GRM. For instance, if the property down the street with gross annual rents of $80,000 sells for $1 million, that's a GRM of 12.5 (1,000,000 divided by 80,000). It's a simple calculation and you can do it for every property you visit. It will give you a sense of what the market says the GRM ought to be for your particular part of the world.

In all likelihood, the offering price of the building will use a slightly higher GRM. Why? Because the seller's broker wants the listing! They want the seller to choose them, so they inflate ever so slightly the price they say they can sell it for. On one hand, they may find someone who falls in love with the property (a terrible idea; I'll talk more about that later) or who just doesn't know any better and pays the asking price. That's a win for both the seller and their broker. Or, more likely, by having a slightly higher GRM, the broker has given their client some room to negotiate down and still get a price they'll be happy with. It's a game, and that's okay—when we get to the section on negotiation, I'll talk about how it ought to be a game where everyone comes out feeling like a winner.

The key thing to remember is the higher the GRM, the longer it will take you to make a profit on your investment.

Potential Rent

One of the things a seller might do that you need to be wary of is that they might determine the value of the building based not on actual rent, but on "potential" rent.

This is a slippery slope.

Let me explain what potential rent is. As I discussed above, one way to get a sense of the value of an apartment house is to add up the annual rent from each unit and multiply it by a certain number. As mentioned, that number could be anything from, say, 7 to 15 (or seven times the combined annual rent to fifteen times the combined rent), and that number can be compared to what other comparable properties are going for to see if you're getting a good deal for the neighborhood and type of property. I explained all of this above, so I'm assuming you're with me. It's not a perfect valuation, but it's a decent, quick-and-dirty way to get a sense of what kind of deal you're being offered.

But sometimes the seller doesn't use actual rents for the basis of their GRM. Instead, they use *potential* rents, or what the annual gross rent for all units would be if they raised the rent. They are assuming that you will raise the rates or that the neighborhood will improve so much that all local rates will increase, or that the value of your property will increase, or some combination of factors, none of which may prove true. And obviously, this extremely rosy potential value of the property creates a much higher sticker price when multiplied by whatever gross rent multiplier they have decided to use.

I am not a fan.

Sure, someday in the future, I assume you will raise the rents. I also assume you've done enough research to have picked a neighborhood that's on the upswing, and that if you keep it long enough, property values will for sure increase. I'm not saying the future isn't rosy. What I am saying is that you shouldn't be paying for possibilities that don't exist yet.

They can argue all they want about the potential of the place, but there's probably a reason they aren't charging the higher rents they want to incorporate into their building's value. Is it more than the market will bear? Are they afraid of losing a lot of tenants if they were to try? It can be tantalizing to imagine the money pouring in from the higher rent you could potentially be charging, but maybe you can't get that. You may not have the same advantages as other places in the neighborhood they may point to because they are charging more. Those places may be comparable in the sense they have the same number of units and they're in the same neighborhood, but they may also have more windows, more green spaces, more square footage, a great manager . . . There are so many variables.

Even if you agree with the seller that you ought to be able to raise the rents soon, you can still negotiate from that. My feeling always is there's a reason the seller didn't raise the rents themselves, and that reason almost always has to do with the investment it would take to make the place worth more to their tenants. For instance, it might take $25,000 to put in new flooring to make the units worth the new rent, to increase the value so people are willing to pay more for it. Is it really potential? If there's going to be outgo before there is a return on investment, you should counter to have that investment taken off the purchase price.

What most brokers do is make two columns: existing rent and potential rent. Brokers will be quick to always give you potential rent; it makes sense, they want the best price for their seller, and also it means a bigger commission for them. That's fine, we're all trying to get a deal. Just understand that the property may already be at its height. For me, I like easy. What is easy to understand is what the rent is. Many owners won't want to take the risk of people leaving by raising the prices, and you definitely don't want to pay top dollar only to have to then spend a lot of money on renovations before you can increase the rent. Be very cautious when the numbers they offer are based on potential and be ready to counter with a number based on actual rents or negotiated down because of deferred maintenance that you will now have to do or renovations that would be required to really make the units themselves as valuable to tenants as the potential rent suggests.

As far as I'm concerned, potential rent is little more than wishful thinking, and while the seller may want to indulge in that, I'm too much of a pragmatist. Multipliers these days are high enough in many neighborhoods that actual rents create a high enough valuation on their own. I don't need to bet on an uncertain future. Pay attention to the underlying number that they are using and don't hesitate to counter with a much more reality-based assessment if you find yourself being offered a value based on potential rent.

Net Operating Income

Another measure to assess an income-producing property's value is to look at the net operating income (NOI). It's pretty straightforward: you take the annual income produced by the property and subtract the operating expenses. This does not include mortgage payments, but does include property taxes, expected losses from vacancies, insurance, and what we'll call "overhead," which includes gardening, maintenance and cleaning, and repairs.

Earlier, I used the example of a $1 million property that had $80,000 in annual rents. Here's what that might look like:

PURCHASE PRICE	$1,000,000
GROSS RENT	$80,000
VACANCY (2%)	($1,600)
TAXES (1.2%)	($12,000)
INSURANCE	($2,500)
OVERHEAD (30%)	($24,000)
NOI (GROSS RENT MINUS OPERATING EXPENSES)	$39,900

Capitalization Rate

The NOI is helpful because you can use it to figure out your cap (or capitalization) rate. This is the ratio between the NOI and the purchase price. Here, you have $39,900 divided by $1,000,000 which is 0.039, or 3.9 percent. This is the rate of return you are getting on your money, exclusive of appreciation (discussed below). As I write this, banks are currently offering savings account rates of under 1 percent, and most are at about 0.5 percent. Traditionally, the stock market has averaged about 2 percent to 4 percent annual dividends if you look at it over the last century. I am not going to give you any advice on what you should do with your money; each investment involves a different amount of risk, and your tolerance for risk is your own business. Personally, however, I would have to take a hard look at this property to see if I thought it was poised to go up. Could I make a difference in how much people wanted to live there by making improvements? Can I negotiate a lower purchase price? That's the beauty of numbers—they provide you with clear information to help you make choices and decisions.

While I disclaim all responsibility for the decisions you make with your money, I will absolutely advocate that you use every tool at your disposal to figure out if a property is a good investment for you. Not everyone can make a go of every property. And some people just want to buy a place so they can take the tax write-off. You need to know your own motives and your own goals. Use comps, GRMs, and cap rates to help you see all aspects of a potential investment.

Appreciation

We just saw that, in our hypothetical example property, you were making a 3.9 percent return on your investment of $1 million. That is a solid rate of return, but it's also not all you are making. While everything else is going on, the value of the property itself is appreciating over time. It may go up in value because of the effort you put into landscaping, repairs, and management, but even if you did very little indeed, historically the value of the property will increase over time. We've seen recently (as I write this) a tremendous spike in real estate values. They will probably come down again, but over the long haul, property values reliably increase.

What this means is that your million-dollar property might increase by 3 percent over the next year (which is typical), or $30,000, so that in a year, it will be worth not $1 million, but $1,030,000. This is over and above your cap rate, and it helps build the equity that will be the foundation for developing your wealth.

Buyer Beware

Ultimately, you have to decide if the property can be improved to meet its full potential, and if the price, whether high, low, or something in between, reflects the cost of doing so. Don't assume a high price means the apartment house has inherently high worth, and by the same token, don't imagine that every building for sale below the market price is a wonderful buying opportunity.

I don't want to scare you off, but I do want to remind you of the adage "Buyer beware." If you see something that's off, believe your eyes, not their excuses. Whatever they tell you must be verified before you count on it. Check and double-check all claims. Talk to experts, talk to people in the neighborhood, and don't let your enthusiasm overwhelm your good sense. Another caveat: only what is written can be honored. Verbal promises are worthless. If the seller promises something, ask them to put it in writing; if they won't, consider that to be a major red flag.

Your broker should be on your side, but especially when you're starting out, you may not know how savvy your broker is. Read all contracts yourself, and if you don't understand something, ask! Don't be embarrassed. Not asking questions because it makes you feel uncomfortable is a sure way to sabotage your future. There's also no shame in talking to a good lawyer who has worked in real estate to help you figure out not just what's in the contract that may need to be changed, but also what's missing from a contract that you want covered. I learned contracts at my mother's knee, quite literally: I was in grade school when I started reading contracts for her. The more you read, the better you get at discovering potential pitfalls and danger signs.

Don't be naive. Question everything and keep questioning until you get the answers you need. You are in business, and contracts are the language of business. Make sure you understand everything before you sign your name.

Reasons I've Walked Away

You're going to have your own reasons for deciding against a certain property, but I thought it might be helpful to give you a window into some of mine.

1. Speaking of windows, a lack of windows is an automatic "no" for me. There's not enough light and not enough

ventilation without plentiful windows. I might be able to rent the unit because it's not something people think about right away, but as soon as the tenant realized how miserable it was, I would lose them and have to start all over again.

2. A bad layout of rooms is hard to overcome. For instance, I've seen lots of places with no dining area in the apartment. People don't want to eat in their living rooms! It doesn't have to be large, but the layout needs to allow for separate spaces. It needs to feel like a home.

3. Similarly, a poorly designed building will be a no-no for me. I have to feel like I want to live there—and not just in the nicest unit, but in every unit. For instance, if the laundry room is right next to a unit, that would be too noisy for that tenant. And it's not something I can fix with a coat of paint; it's a built-in problem.

4. The location of the building may have built-in problems. The first property I did well on was right next to a railroad track. Even though I made money, I vowed never to make that mistake again. I want to own places where people are eager to live, and that means no trains barreling through in the middle of the night.

5. Parking spaces. This is a biggie, especially out here in Los Angeles where everyone needs to drive everywhere. And couples don't just have one family car anymore— families usually have two cars, which means they need two spots. Where are they supposed to put the other car? This isn't true everyplace, but out here, there are lots of streets you can't park on one day a week for street cleaning. I don't want my tenants to risk getting towed every week; no one wants that kind of hassle. I actually saw one place that only had twelve spaces for fifteen units.

Those last three units, without parking spaces, were un-rentable. Move on.

The more properties you look at, the more you'll get a sense of what's good and what's not. Sometimes, I would go out on a weekend and look at three or four properties, never making an offer. My wife, Bernice, would get impatient with me, but if something is not right, it's not right. There are always a lot of properties for sale. Don't be the turkey just because you're a beginner. Take your time, learn as you go. Keep asking yourself, "Will this property suit my lifestyle? Is this the community I want to be part of?" If you're patient enough, you'll find a place that suits you and that has nothing wrong with it that you can't correct. You may pay a certain premium for that, but the premium is worth it.

CASE STUDY

Eighty-Eight-Unit Building

An eighty-eight-unit building was my mother's first property purchased out here in California, and, sadly, the last one she ever bought. It was also a tremendous lesson for me in recognizing when it's time to give up and move on.

The first thing you need to understand about my mother was that she had an incredible tolerance for risk. She was all about buying properties, selling them, getting the capital gains, leveraging her investment, buying bigger and buying more. Once, because of a problem with a contract, she found she'd sold a property before she had bought it—and, no, it didn't end well. But nothing could keep her down. She saw a bargain, not the problems associated with it, largely because she planned to sell it right away and pass the hot potato on to someone else. She was essentially a speculator of apartment houses, and she made money hand over fist.

That was in New York. When I was in my twenties and had moved to California, gotten married, and was in college full-time, my mother moved out here as well. She moved in with me and my wife, and the first thing she did was nose around for an apartment building to buy.

The only problem was that my mother understood New York real estate. She didn't understand Los Angeles.

My mother bought an enormous building, seven stories high, something that looked like the apartment buildings she'd owned back East, a massive, eighty-eight-unit apartment complex. And I don't know, maybe over time she could have found the right buyer for it, but she didn't get the chance. Sadly, my mother was struck by a car and died. The building ended up going to me, my brother, and my father.

This was not a building I wanted to own. The neighborhood had turned, and not for the better. It was too big, it was too burdensome, and there was no easy way to divide it between us except to sell it. Finally, after seven or eight months, I was able to make the sale. My brother and father got their share, and as for me, I took a note from the buyer. This is a practice that can be very helpful, and it may have made the difference between selling the thing and still having it on my hands, but it came back to bite me. Within a year, the L.A. riots were happening, the buyer defaulted on his loan, and suddenly, I had to take the property back. And it was already in a much worse state than it had been when I sold it.

Physically, it had been damaged during the riots; parts of the walls had been knocked in. In addition, the buyer had rented units to some very abusive people, which made it difficult to attract the kind of tenants I wanted in the place. And it made me nervous: I would go to pick up the rent, and the guy would have his gun casually lying out on the table. I want tenants I can have coffee with, without worrying they might wave a gun at me. I ended up running that property for four or five years, doing everything I could to make it work out, until finally, I admitted defeat. I was exhausted. I sold it, but property values had dropped so much, I walked away barely able to cover the bills. But I had to do it. Maybe someone else could make a difference; I certainly wished them luck. I had tried everything in my arsenal and failed. My time and energy were going to be better spent elsewhere.

Never be afraid of sunk costs, that's the lesson here. If something didn't work, I moved on. I never let up. Learn from your successes and from your failures. Don't get sucked into staying because of sunk costs or misplaced ego. This is a business. Come into it as a professional.

CHAPTER FOUR

FINDING PROPERTIES

If there's one thing I really want you to understand, it's that apartment houses are constantly becoming available to you. They go on and off the market all the time. For instance, an apartment complex can become available for reasons including:

- Divorce
- Death
- Retirement
- Partnership breakup
- Foreclosure
- Used-up depreciation
- Change in personal interests
- Property is distressed
- Owner is looking for an exchange opportunity
- And probably a dozen more reasons I haven't encountered.

The thing to understand is that each of these occurrences offers different opportunities and obstacles for you as a buyer.

Let's take divorce, for instance. When a marriage ends, assets need to be divided and often that means property must be sold. But let's look at what opportunities and obstacles this particular circumstance can present. First of all, feelings are probably running high. Divorce is life-altering, and usually not in a pleasant way. You have sellers who are likely not getting along and perhaps not even talking to one another except through their lawyers. This also means that lawyers are likely to be part of the negotiation, and that inevitably slows things down; on the other hand, it is likely that one or both sellers are pushing for a quick resolution and that can work in your favor. They might be more likely to accept a lower price or other terms (such as including, say, the laundry machines at no extra cost) that would make the deal more desirable for you.

In addition, legally, there are probably two equal owners, the divorced couple, who may each have very different feelings toward the property. Maybe one of them doesn't want to sell but can't afford to buy out their former spouse. Could this translate into a partnership situation for you, where you can own half of a larger or more advantageous property than you could afford on your own?

The key in this situation, as with any negotiation, is to try to figure out what the other side needs, and then meet those needs whenever possible in such a way that your needs also get met. Create that win-win. For me, this is part of the thrill: finding a creative way to give the other side what they want so that I get what I want.

When someone dies and the heirs are dividing the estate, it can be just as difficult and emotionally intense for the sellers as during a divorce. When there are multiple heirs, you also have to figure out as best you can what multiple people need from the deal. For the most part, in any kind of family situation or even a professional breakup, at least one seller (and sometimes most or all of them) will have an incentive to close the deal quickly. They want to put this unpleasant moment behind them; wouldn't you? And for this reason, you can often get the price or the terms you want. But at the same time, you may face sellers who have no real understanding of the business or an inflated sense of what the building is worth (this is particularly true of heirs, who may have had no hand in developing or managing the property). This can make negotiation tricky, as they are starting from expectations that are much higher than reality. Just coming down to a realistic price may seem like such a compromise to them that they dig in their heels over what should be the normal give-and-take of negotiations. While there are opportunities in dissolutions, there are also pitfalls to be wary of.

The seller might want to move on because they have used up the depreciation available to them in the property (I'm going to talk about depreciation more in Part Two: Making the Deal). This is someone who is not necessarily interested in managing it as an income property, but in using it to offset their income from other sources. With this kind of situation—as with a seller who is looking to exchange it for a new property because (for whatever reason) it wasn't the right property for them, or with a seller whose interests have simply changed—the deal tends to be pretty straightforward.

The one variable that remains impossible to predict is the seller's personality. Some people come into these deals understanding that it's just a business proposition; my take, for instance, is to create win-win opportunities for everyone. But other sellers go into a negotiation believing that they only win if you lose. First of all, don't be that person. Second, don't play that game with people who are. Once emotions and (worse) egos become involved, the slightest problem can tank the deal. Who needs that kind of headache? To put in all that work only to have someone scuttle it so they can feel powerful? Walk away. And I'll let you in on a secret: as long as you remain professional and levelheaded, the brokers are more likely than ever to remember you. After the seller has blown a couple more deals, the brokers may even convince the seller that your deal was the smart one to take after all. I've had that happen.

If the property has been foreclosed on or is distressed, once again that presents an entirely different set of problems. You have to factor in how much it will cost you to get the property back up to your standards, that's obvious, but you will also have to consider how much time it will take to regain people's trust, to overcome the reputation the building already has.

No matter what the situation, you should always weigh the potential upside with the cost to you in terms of money, time (which includes both the time you put into the property and the time it will take for you to begin to recoup your investment), and energy. Some properties may look like a steal when they really are black holes waiting to absorb your every waking moment and resource. Walk away.

That is part of the power that comes with knowing there will be a constant, ongoing supply of buildings on the market: it gives you the ability to walk away. You have the pen. You have the power. Until you sign the deal, you can always walk away from it, and I believe you should unless you can make an airtight case for this to be a winning deal. Don't be impatient! Every negotiation, even those that fall through, is an opportunity for you to learn what works, what doesn't, what matters to you, what it would take to make a deal that makes sense not just for your bottom line, but also for your vision for the future.

Finding a Broker

Real estate brokers are everywhere. At least, if they're any good, they are probably making a point of being everywhere so that you can find them. Try the Chamber of Commerce, the Lions Club, any nonprofit business group. Brokers are always trying to make connections. If a property is listed, it's listed with a broker, so you can meet them when you are looking at potential properties (which you should do a lot, if you'll remember, because each one can help you identify what you want and what you want to steer clear of).

There are a couple of caveats. First, you don't want someone who doesn't know the territory. Apartment housing is a very specific type of investment and purchase. You want a broker with that kind of training, experience, and sophistication. You can call up a broker and ask if they're in that particular field, and if they are, they can tell you about any property that's in their pocket listing (which means it's exclusively theirs for a short amount of time) or in an open listing, where brokers pool their listings once the pocket term has expired. Finding someone with the correct expertise is essential. There are some terrific realtors who can help you find the house of your dreams; that's not the person to turn to when you're looking for an investment property. You wouldn't go to a heart surgeon for a foot problem.

My second caveat is that if there's any hint of dishonesty, run. This is why you should cast a wide net and try to meet as many people in the real estate and apartment ownership worlds as possible. Word of mouth is invaluable. A personal recommendation from someone you trust is gold.

You may think you can find a property on your own, so why go through a broker? Because they know what they're doing, and you probably don't! Sure, you can find listings online for properties, but going in without a seasoned professional on your side can be disastrous. I've done it myself, but only after I'd already purchased multiple properties, and I still don't recommend it, even for someone with my level of expertise. Why? Because you lose the opportunity to work the negotiations with an arbiter who's an expert in the field. Are you experienced in knowing what to do, how to evaluate the property, how to make comparisons to other properties? Do you think the seller is going to be pliable when it's just the two of you, one-on-one? I doubt it. If they're more experienced than you are, they're probably going to see it as an opportunity to get everything they want from someone greener than they are.

On paper, it looks like you're "saving" the commission; don't think of it that way. Think instead of how your broker is going to *earn* that commission. The broker will find you as many properties as possible to compare, act as a buffer with the seller, write up the paperwork—no easy feat. Today there is so much paperwork to go through to make sure that you are getting the best possible deal that is also legal. You don't want to make a misstep here! The paperwork also protects you from problems that might arise. Do you really want to have to fill it all out without an expert who can explain it to you, who can make sure your interests are covered? You might not even know what to look for or what items are red flags. Look, if you had a toothache, would you go to a dentist or would you want to tie a string around it and pull? The money that the broker gets as a commission is well earned.

What I Look for in a Building

I hope I've made it clear that not every building is right for every buyer. This is a good thing! It means everyone is not fighting over the same three buildings, for one. For another, it means that everyone can bring their own experience, their own touch, their own spark of joy to the buildings they do own.

I do want to give you a sense of what you should look for before you buy, and while some of this is universal, some of it is personal to me. You've been forewarned: your mileage may vary. So here, in no particular order, are some of the things I look for.

1. Neighborhood. Not to belabor the point, but being in the right neighborhood is crucial. I'm not saying it has to be a wealthy neighborhood—that's not my definition of "right." I'm saying it has to be a good fit for you.

   a. Would you live in this neighborhood? Do you feel comfortable? Are these your kinds of people? You're going to be spending a lot of time here and a lot of energy talking to them and helping them feel at home. This is all a lot easier if you speak the same (metaphoric) language and respect one another.

   b. Do you feel safe walking the streets? How about at night?

   c. Is there a grocery store nearby? How about a park?

   d. Think about who would be attracted to living here. For instance, if it's close to a big campus, you might get primarily students and graduate students—is that a population you're eager to serve? Think about what makes them different than, say, a young family with children. They might be transient and need great Wi-Fi, but on the other hand, they don't have babies with colic or need an outdoor play area. There's no judgment here either way; it's just a question of understanding who would be renting in this particular area and how this building either meets or doesn't meet their needs.

2. Do the units have natural light?

    a. Was the building designed so that every unit has sufficient windows or are there "interior" units that have few, if any, windows?

    b. Do any of the windows look out on a wall or other thing that blocks all light? Unless you're on a mountaintop, some windows are going to look out on walls and other buildings. That's not what I mean. I mean do any units have only windows that have no view at all of the sky? If you yourself wouldn't want to live somewhere, chances are you'll have a hard time finding and keeping tenants for it.

    c. What are the local zoning regulations? You really want to know what can or can't get built right next to you before you plunk all your assets down on a place. In this context, check to see if there are any "sunshine" ordinances that might prevent someone from building a monstrosity that looms over your property and blots out the sun.

3. Does the layout of the apartment make sense? People don't really want to live in one big room. They want, if not walls, at least spaces suggesting a dining area and a separate living area, and they likely don't want the only access to the bathroom to be through the bedroom. Walls can be painted, curtains replaced, but an unappealing layout is hard to overcome. Again, imagine yourself living there. Would you be happy?

4. What is the local market for apartment housing? This is twofold:

First, are there enough renters to support the number of units in the area? Second, is the rent affordable? Let's look at each one separately.

a. There is no point in acquiring an apartment building where there are no renters. That's just common sense. What's a little less obvious is how to figure out how many renters a neighborhood can support because neighborhoods change. To give a recent and extreme example, early in the pandemic, people stopped wanting to live in Manhattan. Many people—not all, of course, but enough to have a significant impact on the property market—left the city for less densely populated parts of the country. It doesn't usually happen that fast, but the desirability of neighborhoods does go up and down. A big employer moves in; suddenly, there's a greater demand for units. A big employer leaves and potential renters leave as well. You need to gauge from local "For Rent" signs, conversations with residential real estate brokers, and a good look at the building's books to see if you're going to be constantly hustling to fill the units.

b. What is the going rate for rent? I'm not going to lie to you—at the time I write this, here in Southern California, rental rates are through the roof. This is not, to me, a cause for celebration. Rent used to take up a much smaller percentage of the family budget; now it can easily be one-third of their monthly income. I'm going to touch on this again later, when I talk about managing your building, but now, from a strictly fiscal perspective, beware when rents are too high when compared to income. It cuts into too many other things, including people's emergency savings and ability to save for retirement. You want to offer top-notch housing, but you need to be able to offer it for a price people can afford.

5. Does the building have adequate parking (other than street parking)?

   a. Remember, almost every adult has a car these days. That means you don't need just one parking space per unit, you probably need two.

   b. On a similar note, what parking restrictions are there when it comes to street parking? If a tenant's family comes to visit, are they going to get towed after 3:00 p.m. on weekdays? It's a small thing, but it's an annoyance and you should have your antenna up for annoyances, especially involving cars/parking. They add up over time, making tenants unhappy with their location, which can lead to high turnover rates.

   c. For people in colder climates, what's the access like during the winter? I have a friend who lived in an apartment building in Maryland at the top of a steep hill with a private drive. In the winter, there would be a couple of ice storms every year that brought freezing rain, which would ice over into a thick sheet that was impossible to navigate. This is more of an annoyance for you than for your tenants. Do you have the staff and equipment to make that private drive safe every year? What impact would it have on your liability insurance? These are all things you need to think of before you take on the responsibility of ownership.

6. Finally, how many units are there? The number of units is crucial to your success, not only because rent is multiplied by the number of units you have, but because having more units gives you wiggle room to handle vacancies. A duplex is not as safe an investment as a four-unit complex because when a tenant leaves, you only have one monthly rent check coming in instead of

three. It is, however, twice as good as renting out a single-family home; when you have turnover in that situation, you have zero income until the next tenant moves in. And your expenses, particularly your mortgage, still need to be paid whether you have a tenant or not. I'm not saying more is always better, and I'm certainly not suggesting it's the most important consideration, but it is a major factor in your financial success.

As I mentioned, these are things I take into consideration when looking at a building: neighborhood; unit light, size, and layout; market demand and price; annoyances; and number of units. While you will certainly have other factors that matter to you as well, you can't go wrong taking these points into account.

Part Two
Making the Deal

CHAPTER FIVE

HOW MUCH MONEY DO YOU NEED?

Negotiations

Negotiating is a key part of acquiring any property. Sometimes you are pointing out things that need to be fixed or adjusted to make the deal fair; that's to be expected on both sides. But you should never think of it as haggling for a lower price. Rather, think of it as creating a win for each party. The seller will always want something—money, sure, but also perhaps a quick deal, a long escrow, or maybe emotionally they want this chapter of their life to be over. Finding out what they want and how you can create that win for them is a good way for them to be willing to create a monetary win for you. And saving money is as good as making money. Always look for where to negotiate.

Escrow

A quick word about escrow. I'm assuming that if you are looking to real estate as an investment, you have educated yourself about the basics, including escrow. Just as with buying your home, the escrow agency is simply the agency that carries out the details in the property purchase agreement, including transferring money; pro-rating things like taxes, rent, escrow costs, insurance, etc.; paying fees; writing and recording deeds . . . the list is long. It's also fairly cut-and-dried. Your escrow company will know what they're doing. What's important for you to know is that the escrow office is where the seller will turn over the keys to you, along with the rental resident files once you have become the new owner.

Don't Fall in Love

I believe the biggest difference between house hunting and apartment building hunting is that one is personal and the other is a business. With a house, this is going to be your home. You fall in love with it, you want to make it work. You dream of living there and maybe that makes you overlook a problem with the location or that you'll need a new roof in a year. Or maybe it makes you get into a bidding war with five other potential buyers so you're for sure paying top dollar.

Look, your house is your home. I understand the psychology of it. But emotions have no place in a business decision.

With a rental property, what is your business plan? Is the rent schedule appropriate? How many units are empty and how long have they been languishing? What maintenance has been deferred? What is the overhead? What is the profit? Run the numbers: If the rent is this much, and I put down that much to buy it, I have an expectation there will be a return on my investment. What's left after expenses, mortgage, taxes? Say I put down $250,000 and I make $20,000 a year as my net cash flow—does that give me the 10 percent return I expected? With an income property, making money is the bottom line. If it's not going to make you money, walk away.

If you don't fall in love with the place, you are free to negotiate from a position of strength. All that matters is making the numbers make sense for you; you'll be able to make a deal with the seller or you won't. No hard feelings. There are plenty of properties for you and plenty of other buyers for them.

In other words, kick the tires.

Now, you don't want to be obnoxious about it. Do that and what should be business suddenly becomes personal, by which I mean they won't want to sell it to you. And you need them to want to work with you: while you don't want to pay more than you have to, they don't want to sell for less than they have to. For both of you to succeed, you have to work together (and with the broker, who should be an expert at compromise) to engineer a win-win. I never insulted a seller. But I did ask questions. When was the last time the units were painted? What maintenance has been deferred? Incorporate any legitimate expenses to make a case for lowering the purchase price.

Additional Conditions

In addition to negotiating a lower purchase price, you want to include extra conditions that the seller will take care of (both pay for and complete work on) before you take possession. This will vary from property to property, depending on what needs to be done. These are, however, smaller than deferred maintenance issues; for instance, it's unlikely they'll be willing (or would even have time) to put on a new roof. That kind of request is much better negotiated as part of lowering the purchase price (and then you would be in charge of putting on that new roof once you own the building). But smaller things can give you a spruced-up property on day one and are relatively simple for the seller to accomplish—a good example of give-and-take.

Here are some possibilities:

- Termite inspection
- Interior painting: the halls, any empty units, and/or communal spaces
- Exterior painting: the building itself

- Fixing leaks in any faucets or outdoor watering systems

And there are plenty of others. Anything you notice and legitimately believe brings down the value of the property, you can ask for it to be fixed. You need the right attitude. I've always found that being professional and respectful has gotten people farther than denigrating the property or the seller. But so long as you're respectful, there's no reason not to ask for these things to be addressed. They can always say no.

Let me go back and spend just a minute on the termite inspection. That should always be on your list; it's standard and expected. Probably, the inspector is going to find termites. They may also find other infestations, mold, you name it. But no place is perfect. Problems are to be expected. The key is to find out what the problems are, how extensive they are, and what can be done to mitigate the situation. Always ask for the inspection and to see the inspection report. What you are looking for is that the property has been *cleared* of all termites—you want a clean record.

The seller should always be willing to, first, inspect the property and, second, correct what needs to be corrected. This is true for you as well when you're the seller; sure, there's a cost involved, but delivering the property clear of termites is the right thing to do.

Sticker Shock

Let me give you some potential investments with typical numbers. Warning: reading this may give you a shock! It looks on the surface like an awful lot of money for not that much reward. Hang in there. I wouldn't be writing this book if I didn't believe you could, and should, get in the game.

Example #1: A Four-Unit Apartment House

PURCHASE PRICE	$1,000,000
DOWN PAYMENT (50%)	$500,000
MORTGAGE BALANCE	$500,000
MONTHLY MORTGAGE (4.5% AVAILABLE AS I WRITE THIS WITH 50% DOWN)	$30,396

This is what it's going to cost you to get the building. You are going to put half a million dollars down (again, do not panic! I will talk about how to make this happen later in this section) and you're going to pay the bank 4.5 percent interest on the other $500,000.

GROSS RENT	$96,000
VACANCY (2%)	($1,920)
ADJUSTED RENT	$94,080

This is your annual income from the property. A 2 percent to 3 percent vacancy rate is an industry standard. Obviously, keeping every unit rented out is critical, especially when you only have four units.

Let's look at the GRM. The GRM takes the gross rent, so $96,000, and divides it into the purchase price of $1 million. This gives you a GRM of 10.4. You should look at what else has sold in the area to see if this GRM is in line with (or better than) comparable properties.

Now let's take a look at your expenses:

EXPENSES

TAXES (1.2% OF PRICE)	($12,000)
INSURANCE	($2,500)
MORTGAGE INTEREST	($22,500)
OVERHEAD (30% OF RENTS)	($28,800)
TOTAL EXPENSES	($65,800)

Income minus expenses gives you an annual net cash flow of $28,280.

If you were thinking that owning an apartment building was a get-rich-quick scheme, I hope this disabuses you of that idea. None of my books are about getting rich in a hurry; in real estate, as in everything else I believe in, it takes commitment, elbow grease, and time to build wealth. An apartment complex is an investment in your future.

Let's look deeper at these numbers. First, notice that I only count the interest on your mortgage as an expense, not the full mortgage itself, which is $2,533/month or $30,396/year. I do this because the interest that you pay is the cost of borrowing that money. It is a true expense because you will never see it again. The balance of the mortgage payment, however, goes into the equity of your property. It's money you'll soon be able to leverage into yet another property. It's not gone, just moved into a different pocket, if you will. But it also doesn't mean you don't have to pay the full mortgage. That's why the $28,280 (the $94,080 adjusted rent minus the $65,800 estimated expenses) is called "net cash flow" and not "profit." Note that your net cash flow is almost 6 percent on your $500,000 down payment.

But there's one more number I want you to take into consideration, and that's depreciation. I'm going to go into it in more detail in a few pages, but right now, the key thing to understand is that you can take a percentage of the cost of the building (not the land, just the building) off of your taxable income every year. If you are a high-wage earner, this can provide some significant tax benefits by offsetting your income. Just keep that in mind, because—and you've heard me say this before, it's an all-too-overlooked concept—saving money is as good as earning it.

While we're talking about mortgages, let me suggest that now is a great time to start developing relationships with bankers and making sure you have access to lines of credit. You want to develop your credit before you need it, and you want to foster good relationships with bankers so that you're a person to them, not just a set of numbers.

I mentioned earlier that I never defaulted on a note. This is more than a point of pride to me. It's part of the secret to my success: people trust me not because I'm charismatic, but because I'm trustworthy. What a concept! It's not about how much flash you have, it's about keeping your word over time so that people learn they can rely on you. I've had bankers call me at home after work hours to check on deals that looked a little sketchy to them—"Are you sure about this, Robert? Are you sure about the neighborhood? This other person couldn't make a go of it—are you sure you can?" What they want to know is "Are you sure you won't lose our money?" And, yes, I am sure. I have the expertise, but I also have the track record, not just of making money, but of keeping my word and paying my debts. In this business, that is rare. And it is gold. Be someone other people want to do business with, and opportunities will open up to you.

Example #2: A Two-Unit Duplex

PURCHASE PRICE	$720,000
DOWN PAYMENT (83%)	$600,000
MORTGAGE BALANCE	$120,000

MONTHLY MORTGAGE (AVAILABLE AS I WRITE THIS)	4.5%
GROSS RENT	$48,000
VACANCY (2%)	($960)
ADJUSTED RENT	$47,040
EXPENSES	
TAXES (1.2% OF PRICE)	($8,700)
INSURANCE	($1,800)
MORTGAGE INTEREST	($5,400)
OVERHEAD (30% OF RENTS)	($14,400)
TOTAL EXPENSES	($30,300)

Income minus expenses gives you an annual net cash flow of $16,740. That barely sounds worth it, does it? But here is where depreciation comes in.

Depreciation

One of the great things about buying real estate—or a car, or any other machinery for business—is that from the day you buy it, it begins its march to the junkyard.

Let me explain why this is great.

The tax law understands the concept of wear and tear. Things become obsolete, they break down, they become "used" rather than "new." The resale value decreases over time. When the thing you are talking about is a business asset such as an apartment house, you are allowed to take that depreciation off of your taxable income every year until the value reaches zero.

This is one of the places where I lay out some disclaimers and tell you to talk to a professional tax consultant about this. Why? Because your situation may be unique. There's a certain amount of art to this, not just science. You want to make sure you are only taking deductions that are allowable in your specific circumstance. Not to mention the fact that tax laws change over time. As I'm writing this, the IRS has determined that the value of the building you just bought will go down to zero in 27.5 years; that number has changed before and will probably change again. Consult a tax professional.

Now that the disclaimer is out of the way, here's what depreciation could look like. First, you need to determine what the value of the building is vis-à-vis the value of the land. There are a couple of ways to do this. You could look at it as, okay, what's the land value? This is a pretty easy value to get because your property tax assessor will have some very definite ideas on the subject. You can take their assessment of the land, subtract it from the price you paid for the property, and what you are left with is the value of your building.

Another way to go about it, and one that will almost certainly give you a higher-valued building, is to look at how much it would cost to build that building today. What would be the cost per square foot, material and labor, to build a property with the layout you currently have if you were building it from scratch today? How much would that come to total? Say it was built 20 years ago at $100 per square foot; the price today might legitimately be $200/square foot, so the cost to replicate the building would be double what it had been. That is also, arguably, the value of the building. And in this case, the land's value, instead of being your starting point, would be whatever is left over from the purchase price when you subtract the cost of building the apartment house in today's economy. You can make a case either way; I've known people who choose to be more conservative and those who choose to argue that the value of the building is higher. There's no right answer—there's just what you decide you want to do and, obviously, can make a legitimate case for. You might massage the numbers, but you have to keep it within the bounds of what is reasonable. This is why you want to consult a tax professional; as I said, it is both art and science.

However you determine the value of the building itself, separate from the land, this is what you use to determine your annual depreciation. For the sake of the following examples, and to keep it simple, I'm going to say that the value of the building is 70 percent of the purchase price. So, for the first example I gave you, the purchase for the entire property (building plus land) was $1 million, which gives us a building value of $700,000. Remember that the government says the value will be down to zero in 27.5 years, which means it goes down roughly 3.6 percent every year. Multiply the building value, in this case $700,000, by 3.6 percent and you end up with $25,200. That is how much you can take in depreciation every year in this example. (Note that it's a little trickier your first year, as it might not be a full year that you've owned it, so again, don't try to do this on your own. Consult a tax professional who has experience in this specific field. As with brokers and lawyers, your tax consultant should be an expert in commercial real estate to be truly of value to you.)

This million-dollar purchase was our first example, above, and the net income we anticipated was $28,280/year. You can subtract the depreciation amount from that income, which means you only pay income tax on what's left. In other words, $28,280 (net cash flow) minus $25,200 (the annual depreciation) equals $3,080 (taxable income on the property). This represents an important savings for you. Essentially, the income offset by depreciation represents tax-free earnings.

Taking a look at our second example, the $720,000 property, again assuming the building itself represents 70 percent of the purchase price, we end up with the value of the building at $504,000. The depreciation, at 3.6 percent, ends up being $18,144/year. Our net cash flow from that property (the duplex in Example #2, above) is $16,740; with depreciation, we have a tax loss of $16,740 to $18,144, or a loss of $1,404 every year. What this means is that you will be taking the depreciation off of your entire income, not just the income from the property. If, for instance, you are a high-income earner, an apartment house not only brings you tax-free money every year ($16,740 in net cash flow), but also allows you to lower the taxable amount of your other income by the remainder of the depreciation, or $1,404. I know a lot of doctors, for instance, who find a tremendous tax advantage in taking the depreciation of income properties—which, as I mentioned, is one reason you might find them on the market for no other reason than that the seller has owned them for the allotted 27.5 years and is no longer able to claim the annual depreciation because, according to the IRS, the building's value has zeroed out.

Making a Trade

This brings us to an important point, tax-wise: once the depreciation for a particular building has been used up, you might want to sell it. Now, you might not—it might be the perfect property for you, you may love managing it, by then you will have nearly paid off the mortgage, maybe this is the property that you are planning to build your retirement around. If that's the case, great! The depreciation was icing on the cake for almost thirty years, but you are happy with what is left. On the other hand, if you do want to sell, this is where, without proper planning, that depreciation you took can come back to haunt you. Because, of course, the value of the building has not actually gone down to zero. In fact, it has probably increased. You absolutely must consult a tax professional about potential tax implications before you put it on the market.

But you do have other options. For one, you can use the equity that you have built up in the property as collateral for buying a new property, on which the 27.5-year depreciation clock will begin anew. This expands your portfolio by giving you two properties; you keep the old one and buy the new. You're using the equity in the first as collateral for the loan, which is different from selling it outright. Another option is to essentially trade the property you have for another, larger, income property. It must be larger, more expensive than the one you already own. You're ready to move up. You want to use the equity you've built to parlay it into a bigger apartment house—because I am helping you to build wealth here, and leveraging your equity is a key to that, but also because it is important for tax purposes to trade up. Your smaller property is essentially being folded into a bigger one.

This is rarely a direct swap. Normally, it's a three-way trade, with someone buying your property as you buy someone else's, and it's complicated enough that you want to make sure your broker has some experience in this realm. Your broker will find someone who wants to buy your property for cash, but you will never see that cash; it is instead being used to fund the new property. There is a special kind of escrow to handle these deals. Once the sale goes through, the 27.5 years begins anew for each of the buyers on their newly acquired properties, with the adjusted value of the traded property being taken into account. Again, it's a fairly complex situation with a lot of tax repercussions, including potentially not having to pay taxes on the trade, which is an important consideration. It requires a tax accountant who knows what they're doing. It's called a 1031 exchange and it is beyond the scope of this book, except to let you know that such an option exists and that I've used it many a time.

There are significant and varied benefits to buying an apartment house; these are just a few of them. Your direct benefits will vary. Whether you want to sell or keep your property, always consult a tax professional before making your move. I know it may be difficult to get your head around it, but having worked for the IRS, I can tell you: sometimes, the government doesn't want your money. What they want is for the economy to keep moving smoothly. They want a society that invests in itself and for money to keep flowing. Productivity is terribly important. These tax laws aren't "loopholes"—they are ways to encourage the kind of behavior that keeps money flowing.

Finally, before we leave these two examples behind us, I'd like to point out that putting down $600,000 on a $720,000 building is not what I would suggest. Why? Because it's more than you need to secure a loan and it leaves you cash-strapped to do the things that will improve the property and allow you to up the rent schedule. Let's say you have $600,000 available to you—which you would have to have if that were your down payment. If you put only 50 percent down, or $360,000, instead of the more than 80 percent represented by $600,000, you would be left with $240,000 that you could put to work for you immediately to upgrade the landscaping, repaint the apartments, upgrade the laundry facilities, and lay some new carpeting. Those are the kinds of investments that allow you to charge more for each unit, which is the fastest way to increase your return on investment. Some people get so nervous at the thought of debt that they make decisions that undercut their ability to create wealth. Putting all of your available cash into a too-large down payment so you won't have as much mortgage debt, rather than using that money to increase the value of the property by making it more attractive to renters, is just that kind of mistake.

Investment Analysis

Going back to our two examples, let's analyze our investment:

	EXAMPLE 1	EXAMPLE 2
NUMBER OF UNITS	4	2
PURCHASE PRICE	$1,000,000	$720,000
DIVIDED BY GROSS RENTS	$96,000	$48,000
GRM (GROSS RENT MULTIPLIER)	10.4	15

As I discussed in the section on the gross rent multiplier, this varies widely, largely due to location, but also sometimes because the seller's broker wants the listing and so will list the property at a higher multiple. Looking at these two numbers, for me, a GRM of 15 makes that property much less attractive than the GRM of 10.4 for the larger and more expensive property. In addition, a property that has only two units means that, when one tenant moves out, your income suddenly decreases by 50 percent. You have to assume that units will be vacant sometimes; the problem is, you may not be able to withstand vacancies for very long when each tenant represents such a large percentage of your income. You want to make sure you have funds to tide you over.

Internal Rate of Return

Now let's look at the internal rate of return (IRR), or how long it will take you to recoup your down payment, based on the rent schedule when you first purchase the property.

	EXAMPLE 1	EXAMPLE 2
NUMBER OF UNITS	4	2
DOWN PAYMENT	$500,000	$600,000
DIVIDED BY NOI (NET OPER-ATING INCOME)	$28,280	$16,800
IRR (INTERNAL RATE OF RETURN)	17 YEARS	35.71 YEARS

In other words, even though there is only $100,000 difference between the two down payments, it will take you seventeen years to recoup your down payment from the first property, and nearly thirty-six years to recoup it from the second property. Why? The most obvious reason is that the percentage you put down on the second apartment house was more than 80 percent, whereas it was only 50 percent of the first. But I would argue there's a second reason that doesn't show up in the numbers: putting down a large down payment gives you very little to work with to improve the property right away, which in turn keeps you from being able to charge more in rent. That's not reflected in these numbers, which assume the rent remains constant. I never assume the rent will remain constant; it shouldn't remain constant. You should be putting in expertise, elbow grease, and, yes, money to make the property a wonderful place to live. This will reduce turnover and vacancy rates and allow you to charge more in rent. I talk about this in some detail when it comes to management, but the key to remember here is don't be so worried about debt that you paint yourself into a financial corner from the start.

You should also assess things like square footage and the age of the building. There are many variables in finding something that suits your style of management and is also a good deal. Just be sure not to neglect the basics.

A Word of Warning

You can lose money in real estate.

There are things over which you have some control, like having a backup plan, which might include selling your own house to cover expenses/mortgage/property taxes and moving into one of your own units. You might not like it, but it's an option that can keep you afloat. You can reduce overhead by doing the gardening, maintenance, painting, and cleaning yourself (often with family members, so make sure your spouse or partner is on the same page before you purchase the property). You can manage it yourself. This would be on top of your day job, which you should definitely keep, so you will be spending your evenings, weekends, and sometimes lunch hours handling resident complaints, doing the books, and taking care of, well, everything else. You will be living and breathing your property, possibly for years.

You can still lose money.

Do I think you will in the long run? No. Property has historically increased in value beyond the rate of inflation. Apartment housing also continues to rise, although as I write this, it is rising beyond a rate that I believe to be sustainable. You want your properties to be excellent places to live, safe, clean, and comfortable. You want to be able to keep your rent schedule at the top of the market. But if the market is so overheated that people simply cannot afford rent, that doesn't serve anyone. Eventually, the market corrects itself.

We saw, for instance, the bottom fall out of the housing market in 2008. People suddenly found themselves owing more on their mortgage than their house was worth. What that meant is that people were stuck; they literally could not afford to sell their house. And if they also could not afford a ballooning mortgage payment, they lost everything as banks foreclosed. Don't put yourself in that situation. Be careful what kind of loan you sign up for, think through what you would do if you lost your day job, or if the economy took another hit. In the long run, I believe that property remains a good investment, but that only works if you can actually make it through the tough times and stick around for the long run to occur.

It's also possible you might not be able to make a go of running an apartment house. I was never able to make money from the complex I inherited from my mother. I sold the thing once, only to have it bounce back to me when that seller failed; I sold it again and was happy to be able to walk away, even at a loss. No one can make a success from every property that's out there, and not every person is designed to make a success as a provider of shelter.

When you're buying the property, you will be out a certain amount of money. That's a given. I talk in the next section about maximizing your capital, but no matter how much you maximize, you will have to come up with some down payment. You will borrow the rest of the money in a combination of mortgage and second notes (again, more on them later), and that money you pay interest on. Interest plus principal is how you pay those funds back over the course of the loan; meanwhile, the value of the property is (we hope) improving. This is where you have a fair amount of control: are you going to make things better or not? If not, the value may not rise. It's not magic—you don't just buy a building and suddenly you're a millionaire. It takes work.

Different people want different things out of owning an apartment complex. Some folks are looking to get rich quickly. Let me strongly suggest that this is *not* the way to do it. If you're trying to recoup your down payment just from the rents, well, it takes a long time to recoup $500,000 on $28,280 in net cash flow per year. Some people buy buildings because they want the security; some because they derive great satisfaction from owning and managing to the best of their ability; some because they want the depreciation on their taxes; and others for the pride of ownership. And some do it to create generational wealth, another good reason that takes a long-term view.

When we talk about "getting your money back" in real estate, typically it takes a long time. If you put a lot down, you will be out of debt sooner—and that's good because it means you're not paying interest on that money any longer. But on the other hand, putting a lot down can hamstring you by painting you into a financial corner. Always anticipate needing some funds to improve the property before you can raise the rent schedule.

If you're trying to get your down payment back, that's very difficult in the short run. But trying to get your money back because of what you do with the property, that's a whole different thing. You need to buy a property where it is possible your management can make a difference. Your management needs to be better than what was there before. Your expertise, your willingness to improve the lives of your tenants by improving the property inside, outside, and how it's run—that can make all the difference in the world. Paint, upkeep, changing the lighting, putting in Venetian blinds, replacing the carpet . . . these are all cosmetic, but if the property has been neglected, the cosmetic differences matter immensely. Each thing you do increases the value of the unit to rent.

I plan it out and expect to recoup the investment I put into improvements—not the down payment, mind you, but the additional money I poured into these cosmetic changes—within three to five years, based on the additional rent I can charge for each unit. After that, the rent increases are gravy; they are pure profit, over and above what the net cash flow looked like when I first acquired the building. This, then, might allow me to pay debt down faster, so that I am not paying interest for as long a period, which again means more profit sooner from my initial investment. But it also means that each unit is inherently worth more—that the value of my investment has increased should I decide to sell it, because the unit's value is a multiple of the annual rent.

People like shiny objects. You may see a property that is in excellent condition, already at the top of the rent schedule, and of course it's attractive! The seller has worked very hard to make it attractive. The problem is that there's nowhere for you to go with it. You can continue to keep it nice and to reap the benefits of the work the seller has put into it, but it's going to take a long time for you to see a return on your investment. You don't want a place that's going to need to be demolished, but finding a property that hasn't been nurtured at least gives you a chance to bring it up to your standards. Again, this isn't guaranteed: I've seen people buy neglected property, keep it neglected, and get nowhere with it. On the other hand, I've seen people put very little money down on a neglected property, using that money instead for improvements, who are able to then raise the rent schedule and have tremendous financial success creating a place where people want to live. And I've seen everything in between.

You need to be honest with yourself and think the investment through. Is there room for improvement in this property? What are you willing to do to improve it? Your success is not guaranteed, but by being clear that your job is not just to own a building, but also to manage it better, to improve it in such a way that people are happy to call it home, you can set yourself up for a better outcome.

Chapter Six

Maximizing Your Capital

Raising Capital

You might be familiar with house hunting, and so you know what it's like to put together a down payment and apply for a mortgage. You may also have had sticker shock from looking at the price of houses, especially if you were looking during the early 2020s, as I'm writing this. It's possible that you think you simply can't raise enough money to invest in something even more expensive, like an apartment house—and maybe you can't. But you'll never know if you don't try.

Funds can be available from many sources:

- You can refinance or use the equity from your existing home.
- You can sell your home or use the money you would have put into buying a home and live instead in one of your own units.
- You can parlay an insurance payout or inheritance from an estate.
- You can use any settlement you may have gotten from litigation.
- You can get loans from family members.

- You can get loans from banks.
- You can tap into your savings.
- You can sell stocks and bonds.
- You can look at cashing out annuities.
- You can use your pension distributions.
- You can form a partnership with others and pool your resources.
- You can increase your income with a second job or "side hustle," as it's called these days. You can rent out a room or sell stuff you don't want anymore. Every nickel that comes in should go into a dedicated savings account, earmarked for the purchase of property.

At the same time, you can commit to downsizing your current spending. Many people spend a lot of money on things that don't really give them happiness at the expense of their savings and long-term financial security. Stop trying to keep up with your neighbors or your cousin or your friends! It's not a race! The only prize at the end is that you've frittered away your big dreams on vacations and nights out that fade into memory. If you spend this next year evaluating what you really need and socking every available dollar away, by the time you find the right property, you may actually find yourself in a position to buy it.

Money is everywhere. You just have to have a vision and a goal that motivates you to look for it. You need determination to tap into the possibilities. It takes courage to move out of your safety zone and, yes, it can take work and focus. But you are not pulling in money to hoard. You are not Scrooge. You are doing this for a bigger purpose. You are going to provide housing. You are going to give real people a wonderful place to live, to call home. For me, that was always a calling. Rent is a big chunk of people's income, and they deserve to have a safe, comfortable, beautiful place to come home to at night. At the same time that you are providing excellent value to your tenants, you are building your own financial security and that of your family. This is an endeavor worth your courage, worth your sacrifice.

Not tapping into your resources—and by that, I mean equity, savings, relationships, and ingenuity—is a lost opportunity. Your money can be used wisely to create something special, to make the world a better place, and to secure your family's future.

Other People's Money

I had always had an affection for real estate because land was something I could see and understand. And, as you know, my mother had been a maven for property; I learned from a master. By the time I was graduating college, I wanted to get in on real estate. My wife, Bernice, and I pooled our resources, and in my senior year, we spent month after month looking for a duplex or four-unit apartment house. But the more properties I saw, the more I began to realize that a two- or four-unit building didn't give nearly the rate of return I wanted.

So I started looking for a bigger property. I found one that was eight units. Bernice was not enthusiastic. She knew numbers; she ran them and told me flat out that we didn't have enough money to make the deal. And she was right! Looking at our resources, at the money we had at hand, it was absolutely not enough.

What I did have was other people's money.

This is not to say I went out and robbed a bank. Instead, I looked at the connections I had and how I could make getting this property into a good deal for everyone. Here are some things I have done over the years, and that you can do.

1. At different times, I borrowed money from my brother and my father—and sometimes from both of them together. I know Shakespeare said, "Neither a borrower nor a lender be." I say, baloney. Borrowing money to create something of value to both you and the lender is how you improve the world. My family got a better return on their investment than if they had socked that money away in a savings account. It was a win-win.

2. I went to two of my favorite tenants and offered them a 10 percent discount on their rent if they paid the en-

tire year in advance. Who wouldn't want to pay less rent? Framing it that way gave them a good deal and gave me access to capital when I needed it the most.

3. I would offer the seller their full asking price for the property, but I'd ask them to take a note instead of the full down payment. Remember, I did that as the seller on my mother's property in order to make the deal, taking my portion of the inheritance as a note. Most deals are made with some kind of note. It's essentially another loan on top of the bank loan; on one property, I had six separate notes in addition to the mortgage. Unlike the buyer of my mother's property, I never defaulted on my notes. The people who sold to me received a good interest rate on that money, and it gave me the flexibility to make the deal.

4. I would also ask the brokers to throw their commissions to me and take a note instead, giving me a year to pay them off. Again, they made a good interest rate on that money, and they also helped the deal get made. No deal, no commission in the first place.

5. Once I had income flowing, I would go back to the people who held notes from me and ask them if they'd like to be paid off early at a discount. Again, it was a win-win: if they needed money right away instead of waiting until our contractual deadline, I could provide it. In exchange, I got a discount on the face value of the loan— just like when my tenants were willing to pay me early in exchange for a discount over the face value of the rent. Paying the loan off early also increased the equity I had in the property. What matters in this, as in all negotiations, is creating an opportunity for both sides to walk away winners.

6. Over the years, I developed a line of credit with the bank when I didn't have enough money for a down payment. I was a little naive at first. I didn't understand the value of credit lines. I found out about them through networking. That's another great reason to network: your friends will discover new approaches and you will all share that knowledge with each other.

Regarding credit lines, let me tell you my story. I had a friend who was in my line of business. He was very successful in both apartment houses and commercial properties, and every so often, we would have lunch together. We'd talk about our families and our lives, and sooner or later, we'd talk about our business deals. One day he said to me, "I just got a great credit line through Bank of America." Now, up until this point, I had spurned credit lines. I don't believe in credit cards, so a credit line didn't strike me as something I wanted to touch with a ten-foot pole. But I respected my friend, so when he started talking about credit lines, I was smart enough to listen.

I asked him to explain how it worked. He said, "Robert, they are throwing money out the window. They gave me a credit line of a million dollars." He said you talk to the bankers, give them your financial statements to show them how much you're good for, and then you have to pay it back in a year. I took a little while to think about it, and then I decided, what the heck, I would call up the banker at the B of A and see what the process is like.

The banker was a terrific woman, very smart, and to my surprise, she offered me the same million-dollar credit line. Perhaps even more to my surprise, I took it. It was a new way of manufacturing money. In point of fact, I only needed $850,000 for my next property's down payment, so that's what I withdrew. I knew I needed to pay it back within a year, but when the eleventh month was up, I realized I wasn't going to have the money together to pay it all back. I called up the banker and explained the situation. I really advocate honesty in these situations. Trying to pretend there's no problem is never the answer; it's not just that you're lying to everyone else, which is exhausting, it's that you often end up lying to yourself, which means you're not even looking for solutions anymore.

So, about a month before the money was due, I reached out to her and asked what we could do about it. I'd been in her shoes myself at one point, working for a credit union and helping people who were delinquent on their loans get current again. I wasn't delinquent yet, and I trusted we could come up with a solution together. She didn't let me down. She essentially refinanced the credit line for one more year, and by the time it rolled around again, I was able to pay it back in full.

Investing in relationships, building trust, having a strong financial plan, and reaching out to find win-win solutions—this is the strategy that has served me well all my life, and it served me well here.

Once I had paid the money back—and it was a stretch, but I pulled it off—it proved that I could be relied on. A week later, the banker called me and said, "Now that you've paid it back, I can lend it out to you again." And she did!

Trust me when I tell you we are all swimming in money.

Which is not to say that my wife and I didn't also use our own money. After I had bought that first property, when the deal went through, Bernice and I realized we only had $25 to our name. Even back then, that was not a lot of money! That $25 had to last us until payday at the end of the month. God bless Bernice, she didn't spend a penny. My next paycheck arrived and we were fine. What's important is that that first investment funded the next investment; it was never meant to provide our livelihood. In fact, it was years before I quit my day job.

Don't Touch Your Principal

Speaking of day jobs, this is a good time to remind you how important it is to have another source of income. Don't think of your investment property as funding your daily life. I always structured my investments to stand alone. It was my landlady at a boarding house I lived in soon after I moved out of New York City who gave me that advice. "Never touch your principal," she said. It's fine to spend interest and dividends if you must, but never eat away at your principal or over time you'll have less and less to support your life, your business, and your dreams, my landlady advised. I took that to heart. I've done plenty of things wrong in business, but that one I always did right.

Meanwhile, back to that first apartment house, I had gotten such a good bargain for the property at $56,000, I turned around and put it right back on the market for $58,000. The broker was incredulous; I'd just bought the thing. But I told him, "Don't you think I got a great price for it? Don't you think it's worth more?" He had to agree.

Now, I had already decided that I was not going to be like my mother when it came to buying and flipping properties. I didn't want to speculate. I like owning a property and making the best of it; I know it's just a matter of time until I can increase the value, raise the rents, and start a virtuous cycle of terrific tenants who love living in my units and encourage their friends to rent from me as well. This is gold, and I'll talk about it more when I discuss managing your apartment house later in this book. However, while this first property was a great deal, it was ultimately not right for me. It was a stepping-stone to a property I could really sink my teeth into. Within a year, I had put it back on the market at $58,000, and then I thought, you know what? This place is worth even more than that. We raised the asking price. It was on the market for $62,000 when I found a twenty-unit building that was everything I was looking for, so I upped the asking price again to $65,000, borrowed my brother's share of our inheritance, put my own inheritance in the pot, and ended up doing a deal with the seller where he took my building in trade for his down payment. That extra equity from the increase in value after only a year is what tipped the scales.

The new, twenty-unit property was in a much better location and more convenient for me to be able to take great care of it. Initially, I was only making a 2.5 percent cap rate on it. But it needed a lot of TLC, and I knew that with my improvements, I would be able to raise the rents and attract stable tenants. By the end of the first year, I was making 5 percent. Bernice and the kids and I were still living on my salary, but I felt like the richest guy around. For me, wealth was never what was in my pocket—it was always in the equity I was building. I loved working on my properties; I loved the sense of accomplishment that came from producing something beautiful and useful. That, to me, has always been real wealth.

Put Together a Business Plan

I know you're excited about owning an income property, but before you rush into things, take a step back and put together a business plan. The plan should include actual rent, what the mortgage and property taxes will be, an estimate of utilities (tenants may pay their own, but that doesn't mean you don't need to heat the hallways, run the laundry facilities, and keep the lights on), other maintenance expenses (cleaners, gardeners, maintenance crew), and money set aside for periodic large expenses such as new water heaters and roof repairs. This should all be an obvious first step, a basic spreadsheet of income and outgo.

But there are other items that should go into your business plan as well. For instance, what are other apartments in the neighborhood renting for? If the units at the property on the market are already going for top dollar, it may be years before you can increase rents enough to see a bump in your return on investment. How strong is the market for housing in this area to begin with? Are there plans on the horizon, such as a major employer coming in or an investment in public transportation, that would make the neighborhood more enticing for renters? What are your own plans to increase the value of your property? These usually come with an investment, such as repainting the apartments, improving the landscaping, or adding sufficient parking. How much can you afford to invest, how much additional rent will the investment merit, and when will you start recouping that loss?

You have to have a plan. The more detailed it is, the better. Don't live in fantasy land. If the property will not give you sufficient return on investment (ROI) based on what you can and are willing to do to improve it, it's not right for you. Just because someone can make a go of it doesn't mean you can, or that you can right now. Future you, with more savvy, might be the perfect person for this location, but you aren't there yet. That's another aspect of your plan, your bigger plan: what is the ideal setup for efficiency and to maximize your ROI?

For me, it was five hundred units. Did I know this when I bought my first property? No. But I figured it out within a few years. At first, my family and I did all the maintenance ourselves. I was out there cutting the grass, repainting the units . . . we did it all. But that was never the end goal. If I was going to employ people full time to land-scape, maintain, clean, manage, etc., I needed to have enough units to keep them all employed. I figured out that the magic number was five hundred units, and by the same token, the properties had to all be near enough to each other that my staff wouldn't lose too much time driving from one to another. You have to have a vision. As you learn more about the details (such as how much time your gardeners need, which depends on both the landscaping and the size of your lot, for example, or what it takes to bring an empty unit up to move-in condition), you will adjust. Five hundred units worked for me to maximize cost-effectiveness. You will figure out what works for you.

Your plan isn't set in stone, but just because you'll need to refine it as you go doesn't mean you should fly blind without it, even at the beginning. Put some numbers down. Get used to thinking both big picture and necessary details.

Never, never, never plan to live off of your net income from your apartment building. Not unless you are retired and just need a little extra income, in which case all you're after is one property with a handful of units that you can easily manage and care for. You might even rent out a room in your house or the guesthouse out back and call it a day. Read my book *Retire and Refire: Financial Strategies for People of All Ages to Navigate Their Golden Years with Ease* for more ideas on how to create a secure retirement no matter what stage of life you find yourself in. But if you're planning to build generational wealth, you need to reinvest your profit into your next property and the one after that.

All of my properties were designed to stand alone. We lived on my salary. My side jobs and my investments went to building our savings, which we used to buy our first place. Every property should pay for itself and build equity to parlay into either a better property or an additional one. Other people's money is great, but you need to put up your own money first in order to access it. Hoping for the best and leaping into the unknown is not a viable business plan.

Ask Questions

Closing on a property doesn't happen in the blink of an eye. You show interest, you may even make an offer that they accept, but that doesn't mean it's a done deal. It means now is the time to start digging in, turning over the stones, and making sure the seller is accurately representing the value of the property. It is absolutely critical that you ask a lot of questions. A lot. You are not "bothering" them; you are doing your due diligence and protecting your investment.

Do not be in a hurry to make an offer before you ask all your questions, and if you do make an offer, do not stop asking questions even after it's been accepted. Ask questions of both the brokers and the seller and be very suspicious if they deflect or don't answer any of your questions. You will, of course, ask some questions verbally, but it's also appropriate to ask some of them in writing. Your broker should help you with this; if they try to dissuade you, I would consider that to be a red flag. You have every right, every obligation really, to try to learn the whole picture.

This is your life's savings we're talking about investing. Ask every question you need to until you feel comfortable with the situation.

The first obvious question is: Why is this property on the market? Why are they selling? Is there a personal or business reason for the sale, or is something happening that is having an impact, or going to have an impact, on the value of the property itself?

Is there some legal action being taken regarding the property or anyone involved with the property? Has the city or any regulatory agency issued any kind of demand or request? Are there any ongoing contracts regarding the property? Has there been a major repair or is there the expectation that a major repair will be necessary? Properties might be red tagged for building violations for wiring or plumbing;

there might be earthquake damage or a leaky roof; they may be delinquent in loan payments or property taxes; or other clouds, including poor management or liability suits, may be hanging over the property. Any one of these conditions may require a quick sale for the seller, which can give you room to negotiate. Again, you are trying to meet their needs so they can meet your needs. On the other hand, you also want to be sure you have the resources to handle whatever challenges they'll be leaving on your doorstep.

Not all questions are meant to ferret out problems. You also want to know what personal properties will be included in (or excluded from) the sale. These are things like inside appliances, outside furniture, laundry equipment, or other equipment or tools. This is one of the things you want in writing. I once had someone take all of the laundry equipment with them, completely stripping the laundry room, even though we had contractually agreed that it would be part of the sale. I told him to return it and he couldn't—he had already sold it! He had to buy me all new equipment. You can't anticipate what someone will grab on the way out, but you can protect yourself financially by spelling everything out ahead of time.

This list of questions is by no means exhaustive. You should ask absolutely everything you can think of. Their inability or unwillingness to answer any question should be your cue to dig even deeper into the issue. Sometimes you won't like what you hear, but you'll still be willing to move forward. That's fine; forewarned is forearmed. Other times—and especially if they prove to be misrepresenting anything—it's a sign to walk away.

Debt

Before I start talking about ways to maximize your capital—which means leveraging all the resources at your disposal to get a property that will be a real stepping-stone on the path to building wealth—I want to talk to you about debt.

You've probably spent the last several years trying to get out of debt. If you haven't, you might want to do so now. Never carry a balance on your credit card—more on that in a minute—and pay off your car, your student loans, your mortgage. For the car and the student loans, it may be too late to do anything about it, but if you're young or you have children, let me recommend 1) rethinking going into debt for an education, and 2) designing a life that is fulfilling without being a money suck.

Let's take education first. Where can you go to school for little to no money? Depending on your family income, that might mean a state university, or even a couple of years of community college first. Or it could mean an Ivy League school; most of them give full financial aid to families making under a certain threshold every year, and if you've got the grades, why not give it a shot? But going into significant debt for an education stifles your freedom after you graduate. If you have to take a job, any job, to pay off the debt, you can't necessarily take the risks or enter the field that would give you the most satisfaction and growth in life. And with that debt hanging over your head, you also won't be in a position to invest in yourself and your dreams for years, sometimes decades, afterward.

As for your lifestyle, it is built on a series of decisions that can either develop your nest egg or dribble money out of your fingers. This is probably not what you want to hear; after all, you're reading this book because you want to create wealth! And I want you to do that. I remember the day I got my Jaguar. It represented to me the pinnacle of success, that I had made it as a businessman. My heart still fills with pride thinking about that car. I want you to have that moment as well. But that moment came after years and years of living frugally. My wife and I ate in, took walks in parks, watched TV instead of going to movies . . . the list is endless. We never tried to keep up with the latest trends, whether in clothes or cars or technology, because we had a bigger vision for our money. Socking away every dime gave us the ability to make the most of it when opportunity presented itself.

Don't think of it as depriving yourself—think of it as investing in your future. To use one major expense as an example, take your car. You don't need new, you don't need fancy. You need something that will get you to work without breaking down. When that's your criterion, instead of how impressive you'll look behind the wheel, you gain a lot of flexibility in terms of finding solutions.

How does this relate back to debt? First of all, if you are in debt, get out of it. Get a safety net in place and then start building your investment pool. The freedom this will give you mentally as well as professionally is untold. If you are already out of debt, or mostly out of debt (your mortgage is not a major concern to me, provided you have equity to work with in your home), good for you. But even you may require rethinking some assumptions.

For instance, whether you've already succeeded in getting out of debt or not, you have probably been trying to get out of debt for a while now. As a society, we carry so much debt, it's absurd. According to the Federal Reserve Bank of New York, Americans carried a total of $807 billion in credit card debt alone in 2020. You may have gotten out of that hole, and here I am, telling you to look at properties that will for sure plunge you back into debt, possibly more debt than you've ever carried before.

Do not panic.

There is good debt and there is bad debt. I promised to talk about credit cards, and here's where I pull no punches, because as far as I'm concerned, that's the worst kind of debt. The first problem is the kinds of stuff you decide to go into debt for with a credit card. You don't need the newest tech, the fanciest vacations, or a "refresh" of your interior décor on an annual basis. You don't need to be out on the town. Look, I'm a fan of networking, but that's not the same thing as happy hours or expensive dinners with friends. Golfing is the stereotype of how people do deals, and for all I know, it's how rich people do them still, but I never did. I found that being honest and figuring out how to help other people was a better way to network and without country club fees. You're trying to build something, and you can't do that if you're frittering away your money on things that vanish in an instant. Learn to cook if you like fancy food! That's a skill you'll have for life, not just a steak that'll be eaten in a blink.

But even when the credit card expense is something like, say, business cards or even inventory, I'm still not a fan. Why? Because when you buy something on credit, no matter what it is, you are buying it with expensive dollars. Unless you pay off your credit card every month, you are paying an exorbitant interest rate on those purchases. Your APR, or annual percentage rate, can range from around 16 percent to a whopping 25 percent. It doesn't look like much at first, a few extra dollars a month, but it will add up over time. Think about it: would you really buy that new TV if it suddenly cost 15 percent to 25 percent more than the sticker price? Of course not. I'm betting you wait for sales to make big purchases; you might even cut coupons for your groceries. But if you put those things on a credit card that you don't pay off every month, it's doing you no good at all because the dollars you are using to buy them with come with a price tag all their own.

Credit card interest is the low-hanging fruit. Don't buy something you don't actively need, and when you do buy something, make sure you can afford to pay in full that same month. Curbing your dependence on expensive credit will free up financial resources for bigger and better things . . . like buying an income property.

Income property is good debt. It is the kind of debt that makes the most of your creditworthiness. The interest rate on a mortgage is far less than that on a credit card: around 5 percent instead of 15 percent to 25 percent. It *looks like* more because you're borrowing more money and so you notice it. You can't help it. Suddenly, there's a new monthly payment you have to make, and it's going to be sizeable. This fear of going into debt, or back into debt if you've already paid off the mortgage for your own home, can keep you from making a bold deal, and that is a real shame.

Let's start by taking a look at the mortgage you already may have, the one for your house. For many people, paying a monthly mortgage has been normalized. You would have to pay rent anyway, right? You have to live somewhere. And paying a mortgage monthly, you've probably been told that it's like paying yourself rent. I don't disagree. I own my own home—I understand the desire to have your own place and also, as a businessman, I can see the value in having equity that you can leverage. What hasn't been normalized is the idea of paying a mortgage for an income property. And yet, your own home doesn't bring in income. All that "paying yourself rent" stuff? It's not the same as getting rent from someone else. You are building equity, but if you're not doing anything with that equity, it's not building wealth the same way an income property can.

Paying a mortgage on an income property is a big step, but just as when you pay the mortgage on your home, you are building equity you can later leverage for something even bigger. In addition, you are getting income from tenants, which should:

1. Cover the mortgage payments

2. Cover your operating expenses and property taxes

3. Provide some additional yearly income to plow back into your investment business, helping you to purchase even more (or better) property down the line.

It can also give you a backup plan if other things go wrong. For instance, if you lost your job, you could sell your home and move into one of your own units, keeping a roof over your head as well as money coming in while you get back on your feet. That's what an apartment house has over the family home: it can provide income in a pinch. Would I rather you use that income to build your future? Sure. But in desperate times, having income tenants and a place to live beats trying to piece together a slew of part-time jobs or scrambling to find a room-mate, hands down.

Good debt builds equity in a business. Bad debt keeps up with fashion trends or conflates building happy memories with blowing a wad of cash. Know the difference.

Minimize Your Down Payment

Speaking of debt, there are reasons you might want to minimize your down payment, even if it means taking on more debt at the start. Let me explain.

A smaller down payment means that you have more money at

hand for better purposes than minimizing your debt. I don't want you to keep the extra money in a savings account, mind you; I want you to put it to work.

Let me give you an example:

PURCHASE PRICE	$1,000,000
DOWN PAYMENT (50%)	$500,000
LOAN BALANCE	$500,000
FIRST YEAR'S INTEREST ON LOAN (AT 4%)	$20,000

With an investment property, you might think you need a 50 percent down payment. But everything is negotiable. And, in fact, I'm going to show you right now why you might want to put less down and negotiate a bigger loan. In any event, you'll want to talk to your bank. What are their parameters? Talk to your broker—see if they will take a note on their commission. Talk to the seller—see if they're willing to take part of the down payment as a note. Don't let the fear of having to come up with a down payment (of any size) keep you from exploring your options.

Finally, I'm going to use 4 percent as a mortgage interest rate, just as an example; interest rates are sure to be different when you read this book from what they are as I'm writing it (in fact, they'll probably have changed by the time I finish the book). But we have to use something as an example, and this gives you an idea of the relative numbers. Let's see what happens when you decrease your down payment and increase the amount of your loan:

PURCHASE PRICE	$1,000,000
DOWN PAYMENT (30%)	$300,000

LOAN BALANCE	$700,000
FIRST YEAR'S INTEREST ON LOAN (AT 4%)	$28,000

At first glance, you might only see the extra money you have to pay in interest. But what I want you to see is the cost of that money. You are paying an extra $8,000 that first year in exchange for an extra $200,000 to use for a better purpose than paying down your debt. Sure, $8,000 of it will go to interest, but that other $192,000? That can be used for upgrading the property, which in turn will allow you to charge more rent and/or increase the value of the property, which will increase your equity. It could be used to buy the next property, or maybe it's the buffer you needed to be able to make this deal to begin with. It could also be used for an emergency; you should never be stretched so thin that you can't fix the roof or put in a new hot water system. The last thing you want is for the property to go downhill through neglect because you can't afford to improve or even maintain it to reasonable standards.

You want to attract reliable tenants with top-notch apartments that will go for market value, and it will almost certainly take an investment of time, energy, and money to bring the property up to spec. A higher loan payment will cut into your net profit, but it can actually lay the groundwork for much higher profits down the line.

This isn't quite minimizing the down payment, but there is some wiggle room around when your first mortgage payment is due. Typically, your first payment is due thirty days after the first month you've owned the property. If you close on the fifteenth of June, your first mortgage payment is due not on the first of July, but on the first of August. This means you can collect July's rent before you have to pay the August mortgage. But you could also ask the lender to start the loan payments a month later. I've done it with lenders I knew and had worked with; this is why treating people with respect and never defaulting on your loans makes excellent business sense.

In those times when I did need a little wiggle room to smooth out my cash flow, I was able to get it. I once needed extra time to pay off a big loan, a million-dollar loan, and I was able to convince the lender to give it to me, because she knew from past experience that I didn't default on loans. I also didn't engage in magical thinking. I had a plan for how I would be able to pay it off and I had a reputation for following through. I had never once misrepresented a situation to her, so she trusted that I wasn't full of hot air now. For all the stereotypes of the greedy banker, they don't want your property; they want their loan paid in full. It's a lot less hassle that way! But they're also not there to solve your problems for you. You have to have a plan to make the numbers work out for both of you, and you have to have a stellar reputation and (ideally) a long-standing relationship as a foundation.

So what are some ways to minimize the down payment? Your first line of defense is to negotiate how much the property is going to cost you to start with.

Negotiate the Purchase Price

It is critical to negotiate the purchase price down, and for reasons other than, obviously, you want to pay less for the property overall. When you negotiate the price down, it gives you ammunition to go to your lender and say, look, this property is valued at $1 million, but I'm getting it for $850,000. That means there's already $150,000 in equity the moment I take ownership. Can you cover a higher percentage of the asking price, say 60 percent instead of 50 percent, given that there's so much equity already embedded in the property?

They may say no. But they might say yes. This is a reason for you to be impeccable with your credit now: to give you credibility later. The other reason they might be willing to cover more of the loan—once you give them a legitimate reason to consider it—is that they know and trust you. Like every business, real estate is a business of relationships. When I find a lender I like, someone straightforward and competent, I use them for everything. They get to know me and to trust I will not default on my next loan because I haven't defaulted on prior loans.

Just to give you some context, I used to work for a credit union; in fact, my mandate was to clean up the high default rate on loans! I did that by treating people with respect, setting up payments they could manage, and making expectations clear. I understand both sides of the table. Bankers are human beings; they want things to go well so they don't have the headache of paperwork or colleagues second-guessing their decisions. Just like us, they want to work with people they trust. Be that person in every interaction, and they are more likely to give you the benefit of the doubt when you need it to close a deal.

You need to be careful when you negotiate the purchase price down. You never want to be disrespectful, but you do want to point out reasons why the price is a little too high. You can point to comparable properties that have recently sold for a lower price. You can remind them of deferred maintenance that you will need to do because they didn't. You should never make it seem like the property is a hellhole (if it is, I don't advise making an offer in the first place), but you can respectfully kick the tires a little. The initial purchase price is usually above what the broker really thinks they can get, because it gives them wiggle room. In the same way, you should counter with a price that is lower than what you'd be willing to pay so that you, too, have room to negotiate—up in your case, down for them. Don't be disrespectful or they won't want to sell it to you at all, but so long as you're professional and not insulting, hey, it's a dance. Both sides should understand that.

Another way to limit your down payment is to ask the seller to take part or all of the down payment as a note, or loan, on the property. You can ask either or both brokers to take their commissions in notes as well, plowing that money back into the down payment. I'm going to talk about this strategy a little more in a minute.

Create a Win-Win

A way to approach negotiations that has been successful for me (although, given our competitive culture, it might sound counterintuitive) is to try to make every negotiation a win for both sides. Never go in thinking you have to "beat" the other person. You need their cooperation to make your ambitions come true, so why would you frame it as "beating" or "winning" or even "losing," for that matter?

You get something you really want; they get something they really want. You both won't get everything, but you'll each have the key to moving forward with your own individual lives and businesses. If your success depends on their failure, you are not somebody I would want to work with or even rent from, for that matter. That's no way to build a business or a life.

And it won't help you in the long run. What people don't understand is that when you create an adversarial relationship, you create an adversary. Suddenly someone who didn't know or care about you, or might even have wished you well, suddenly has an emotional stake in your failure. And that's because you went in like a bulldog and created that dynamic. You lose the opportunity to get what you really want when your ego demands a petty "win."

Luckily, it doesn't have to be that way. Instead, go into every negotiation with the goal of trying to meet the seller's needs. One thing everyone wants is to work with someone they can trust, but also someone they can work with. I can't even believe I have to say this, but be straightforward and respectful. Be a professional. I have had sellers reject my offer in favor of someone else who offered a higher price, only to reach back out to me because that buyer was arrogant, tried to take advantage of them, or lied about their assets.

So how do you figure out how to make it a win-win?

First off, you have to figure out what would make it a win for you. Take a look at your plan. What are things that could help you increase the value of your investment or decrease the amount of money you have to put down? Are there necessary repairs they can credit you for? Would they take part of the down payment as a note instead? Can they accommodate your need for a longer or a shorter escrow? Is there something about the property or the deal that to you would be a deal-breaker, and can they work with you on that? Know what would be essential for you, what would be nice, and what you don't care about at all—in other words, where you would be more than willing to help them out. You're not sharing this with them, mind you. To some extent, a negotiation is a psychological dance. It would be great if both parties could just say up front what they need and what they're willing to offer to get it, and everyone could walk away happy, but that's not human nature. What I want you to do is to go in knowing yourself, where your line in the sand is and why. It should always be for the good of the business, never for the good of your ego.

Having figured out what you want, the next step is to figure out what the seller wants. Part of your job as a real estate investor is to find out what makes the seller tick. "Why are they selling?" is the first, most obvious question. Are they selling the property to have enough of a stake to buy a bigger place that has just come on the market, and if so, does that mean they need a shorter escrow so they can make that deal? Is it essentially an estate sale where the heirs have no time or interest in the finer points and just want a quick and simple transaction? How can you meet their needs, whether emotional or professional?

I promised that I would talk about the fact that a seller might take back a note on the property in lieu of part of the down payment. A broker might do the same on their commission. Although it's something that might help you stretch your cash, this is not a favor they're doing you, and I don't want you to think of it that way. A note is a loan and that means there is interest on that loan monthly. For a seller (or a broker), what you're giving them is steady, predictable income for, say, the next five or ten years, with a clear return on their investment. For the seller, it's a way to continue getting steady income from the property without the hassle of actually having to manage it. Some people won't be interested, which is fine, but for others, this meets a financial need for steady, long-term income. It's your job to show them the upside of this opportunity. They're grown-ups; if it doesn't work for them, they'll turn you down. If you can't do the deal without a note (or multiple notes—I've had as many as six notes on a property, not counting the mortgage!), then you walk away and they find another buyer. It's not personal, it's business.

A note is one thing that might meet both of your needs. Although the number changes at different times, a market rate on a second trust deed (in other words, a note) is often between 8 percent and 10 percent, which is currently far more than they can get putting the money into a savings account. It's useful for you to know what they're going to do with the money (either from the sale, if they're the seller, or from the commission, if they're the broker) once they get it. If you can offer them a way to make more money from that money, do it! They're allowed to say no if it's not right for them. The nice thing about working with a seller or a broker is that they know how valuable the property is. As long as you are a person of integrity, they can rest easy that a note to you is a solid second that they don't have to worry about.

Knowing what they want and being able to offer it can give them incentive to bend on things that matter to you. Let's take purchase price. You might think that purchase price is the one thing where one of you would be a winner and the other a loser, right? Wrong. The initial purchase price is usually a little higher than they expect to get, because they anticipate having to negotiate it down, but I once offered a seller their full asking price, no negotiation. They were thrilled! What did I get in return? They took a note on my down payment so that I paid them over several years rather than right away. It meant I could afford the property, one on which I knew I could make a lot of money, without having that money in hand. And the thing with notes is that people's needs change. They may be happy to have that steady, reliable income for the first couple of years, and then an opportunity may come their way where they need a significant chunk of cash up front.

I always reach back out to people holding my notes a couple of years in, when I have the money to cover it, and I offer to pay off the loan at a discount. They can always say no, and sometimes they do, and I keep paying monthly until the note is covered. But more often than not, they are eager to get their hands on the bulk of that money immediately instead of waiting for the term you agreed upon to be over. Their needs have changed, and you are now in a position to help them while at the same time building equity for yourself.

When someone has taken a note from you—in other words, they have given you a loan that you are paying back with interest, usually in monthly installments—you want to look at a couple of things. First, how much is the note? Do you have the money to pay it back? It's not unusual to have, say, the seller take back a note on all or part of the down payment. It's a way for them to continue to get monthly income from the property they just sold, only without having to do any of the work managing or maintaining it. It can be a win-win for you both right there. It's also not unusual for you to be cash-strapped when the deal is made, especially if you are investing in improvements on the property once it's yours. But once you are able to increase the rent schedule and start filling any vacancies, your property now being much more attractive to potential tenants, money will start coming in and you may soon be in a position to pay off the notes early. So that's the first thing: when the dust of the deal settles and you find yourself in a stronger financial position, look at how much the note is and whether you can afford to pay it off now. Don't try to do all the notes at the same time; look at each of them one by one.

When you have a note that you are in a position to pay off, you next want to evaluate whether or not you actually want to pay it off. Was the other party trustworthy during the deal? Is there a way to offer a win-win? Often when someone takes a note, they have no need of the money in the moment, but life changes. I had one guy take back a note from me, only for him to have an opportunity a few months later to use the money for more than twice the return he was getting from me. He approached me about paying the note off early. I said I would, at a 15 percent discount; he countered with something like 7 percent, and I responded that I couldn't do it for less than 10 percent. Deal. It really can be that easy.

Another time, the sellers were a group of doctors, each of whom had taken one-sixth of the note. Do you know what that meant? It meant the amount each one held as a note from me was peanuts compared to their income. I went to them and pointed out that it wasn't worth the time and effort to collect the monthly payments from me for the next couple of years—how about if they gave me a 10 percent discount and I'd pay everything off in full right now? Again, done. It made sense to them. The 10 percent discount was worth not having the hassle of the outstanding loan, and I made 10 percent on the deal.

A brother and sister, as sellers, held another note from me, and she was very happy with the monthly payments while he was eager to give me a discount and get paid out now. We split the note in half; why not? Everyone got what they wanted, and if I couldn't get a discount on the entire amount, I was very happy to have half of it discounted.

Another woman, a very sweet lady, took a note from me. I heard that her son was in debt at a terrible interest rate, so I went to her and offered to pay it back immediately at a discount so she could help her son pay off his loan and save him from the exorbitant interest. Of course she said yes. Win-win.

Life changes. The other person may have a sudden need of the principal, and you are always interested in getting a discount on what you owe. You need the tenacity to always be looking for deals, to keep going back; you made a deal to get the note, which gave you the ability to buy the property, now you can go back in and make a new deal to repay it and give you instant equity you can leverage later. It's the thrill of the game, and it's also good business to always be taking action.

Playing Hardball

Sometimes, you'll get a seller who wants to play hardball. Maybe they are heirs to the property and don't really understand the game. Maybe they are going through an ugly divorce or maybe they believe that the original price is what they deserve. Let's say that for whatever reason they are not willing to budge, or they'll budge very little, on the purchase price. What do you do?

I have three suggestions for you.

1. Develop a relationship with both brokers. Again, this is a business of relationships. Don't badmouth the seller, mind you; that'll just make their broker look bad. And you are not interested in setting up a confrontational relationship. You don't want either broker to have to "pick sides"—this is not high school. Instead, be professional. Continue to show interest in the property. Enroll both brokers in your vision of what the property could be. You are genuinely coming into this because you believe you can make money, sure, but also because you believe you can create a wonderful place for people to live. (If that's not always your vision, there are other ways

to make money that might be more suited to your life. Go check out my other books, especially the second one, *Building Wealth 101*.) Sharing your vision, both as a businessperson and as someone who is creating a wonderful housing experience, can help get both your broker and the seller's broker onboard.

2. Look at the property's needs. If the seller did agree to your offer, what would you do with that extra money? Has there been deferred maintenance? Does the roof need repair? When was the place last painted? Is there anything they could throw in that you would genuinely want? See if they'll negotiate down the cost of any repairs or upgrades and ask for absolutely everything you want. Sometimes sellers need to see that you are not just trying to take advantage of them, but instead have valid and specific reasons for disagreeing with them on the asking price.

3. Run the numbers. If the higher asking price does not make financial sense for your business, if it will impact your ability to put the deal together, or if it would take too long for you to recoup that higher investment, walk away. Be regretful, don't burn bridges, but make it clear that you will not be taken advantage of. It may not help you with that seller, but that's okay. You're playing a longer game. If you have treated everyone with respect, both brokers will remember you the next time a suitable building comes on the market.

You can also ask them to make repairs before you take possession. If they're not willing to lower the asking price so that you can, say, repair the gutters or put in a new sprinkler system, will they do it instead? Will they repaint the hall, repair the steps, put in new siding, fix the leaky sinks? What else would they be willing to throw in? What equipment do they have that they might be willing to leave behind for you? How can they get their asking price and you get in exchange things you would otherwise have to pay good money for after closing?

The Psychology of Numbers

Retail marketing psychology suggests giving discounts to consumers. Why? Because it makes them feel as if they have gotten a bargain, that they have "put something over" on the seller, that they have won. But that is just an emotion created by the seller. The original price is marked up so that it can be marked down without the company losing money on the sale. They'll sell a few at full price to people who are in a hurry or otherwise motivated to buy immediately, and that's gravy. But most of their profit will still come at the lower price when the bulk of their sales will be made. The customer feels like they're getting a bargain, but in fact, they're being played. They are getting whatever it is—clothes, car, electronics—at the company's preferred price point.

The same basic principle is true in real estate.

It's more complex, of course, but the basic idea that brokers will inflate the price to give them room to negotiate down still holds. Where it gets complicated is that the seller may not be fully aware that the price is inflated. They may have chosen the broker who "promised" them the highest asking price without fully understanding that the asking price is not always the purchase price. Your job there is to help move the seller's expectations downward without throwing their broker under the bus. The seller might also have an emotional attachment to the property, or they might have financial needs that only the highest possible sales price can meet. You need to understand both the seller's business needs and their emotional needs if you're going to negotiate a reasonable deal.

On their end, the seller is using psychology on you. They may either inflate the asking price so that in the end you'll feel, like a consumer does, that you are getting a bargain, or they may offer the property at a price below market value in the hopes of drawing in several interested buyers and creating a bidding war that will drive the purchase price way up. This is a very tricky situation to be in. You need to be careful. It's psychological: buyers feel like they could be getting a great deal, so they jump in, only to then be caught up in the competition and end up bidding more than they would have been willing to pay as an initial asking price. It becomes a game, an ego thing, where it's as much about "winning" as it is about acquiring the property. You need to dispassionately work out how much you would be willing to pay for the property, how much makes sense from a business point of view, and stick to it no matter what if you're going to jump into it with the rest of the sharks. It is very hard to resist the energy that comes from a feeding frenzy.

Once you buy a property there will almost certainly come a day when you, too, become a seller. That's why it's important for you to understand both sides of the coin. As a seller, you want to be aware of your own emotional attachments or desire to win, and put it all aside for the good of your business. Recognize the psychology involved, but don't let it drive your decisions. You may work with buyers who place value on the style of the property or its history or reputation. They may fall in love with its layout, color, or individual apartments. All of these truly matter to them, and you can meet those needs in exchange for them meeting the needs that matter to you. And sometimes, you will find someone who wants to buy to satisfy their ego. That, too, is good information when it comes to negotiating a deal that works for both of you.

Stretching Your Dollars

Here are a few tips for stretching the money you need to come up with for the down payment. First, you should try to close on the third of the month. Why? Because rent is paid on the first of the month, and it's paid in advance for the next month, not for the month that just passed. By the third of the month, the seller should have collected the rent for a month in which you will own the building. In other words, the seller now has a significant amount of cash that belongs to you. Does the seller want to hand you that cash? No, they probably don't. A win-win is for them to sign that money over to you as credit on your down payment. I always ask to close on the third of the month so that the amount I have to put up is reduced by the rent I am credited for. They still end up with the same amount of money, some of it now being directly in their pocket, which generally makes people happy. As for me, rather than have to find that last, say, $25,000 before the deal closes, I simply get credit for it. Instant equity.

Equity

Equity in your property increases in two primary ways. The first is simply arithmetic: as you pay off your loan(s), the amount of the property that you own outright increases. This is equity. Every payment on your mortgage decreases the amount you *owe* and increases the amount you *own*. Your early mortgage payments are mostly interest, but some of that money does go to paying down the principal. As the payments continue, less of the money is interest (because there is a little less principal generating interest every month) and a little more goes to paying down the principal even further, until finally your last payment pays everything off. Right? Simple math. Every mortgage payment buys you a little more equity.

Here's an example: You buy an apartment house for $1 million with 50 percent down and 50 percent financed. Your bank loan is $500,000 and your monthly mortgage is, with today's numbers, something like $3,000/month. This number will inevitably have changed by the time you read this, but it gives you a sense. At first, most of that $3,000 goes to paying the interest on the loan, but if it *all* went to just paying interest, you would never pay off the loan, right? So a portion of it, a fairly small portion at the beginning, goes to paying off the loan itself.

Let's make up some numbers here. Let's say that $2,500 goes to the interest and $500 of that first payment goes to the loan. This is all made up, just to keep the numbers easy to see, but the idea is right. Because you paid off a little of the principal, the next month, your loan amount is $499,500. Your payment is still $3,000, but you are paying $4 less in interest the second month than you were the first, so an additional $4 goes to paying down the loan in month two, or $504 goes to the actual principal. By month three, your loan amount is down to $498,996. Congratulations! You now have $1,004 in additional equity (above your down payment) in the building. You are on your way, month by month, to building enough equity for leveraging your current income property into a bigger and better building.

The second way equity increases is usually much more dramatic. I touched on this earlier when I talked about appreciation. Historically, real estate increases by roughly 3 percent per year, compounded. In some markets, it can increase much more rapidly—but it can decrease rapidly, too. Beware of the bubble. Still (and with all the usual warnings that past performance is not a guarantee of future earnings) over the long haul, real estate values have reliably gone up. When the value of your property increases, so does your equity.

Let's take a look at that hypothetical $1 million property. To keep it clear what we're talking about, let's assume you put down $400,000 and got a mortgage for $600,000. With that down payment, you already have $400,000 in equity. Now let's watch what happens over time. At 3 percent compounding interest, after one year, the property is worth:

$$\$1,000,000 + 3\% \text{ of } \$1,000,000 \text{ (or } \$30,000) = \$1,030,000$$

This is just from increased property values alone. In other words, not counting the gain from the mortgage or from any improvements you might have made. Your equity in the building is no longer the $400,000 you put down, it's:

$$\$1,030,000 - \$600,000 \text{ (mortgage)} = \$430,000$$

That equity happened without you putting any money into it. It's not a reflection of how much you paid down the principal, but merely how much more that same property is now worth. And the interest is compounding, so the second year, the property isn't just worth another $30,000, it's worth:

$$\$1,030,000 + 3\% \text{ of } \$1,030,000 \text{ (}\$30,900) = \$1,060,900$$

Which means your equity is now $1,060,900 minus $600,000: $460,900. That is an increase in equity of almost $70,000 over two years, or a whopping 17.5 percent. Where else will you get that kind of return on investment? Because property values increase, your equity grows by over $30,000 a year, and by ever-increasing amounts each year, over and above what you're getting by paying down the mortgage.

This is nothing to sneeze at. I mentioned earlier that I once used the equity in one property as a down payment for another, better, larger property—essentially, the seller and I swapped properties. Especially if you were able to get a deal as I was, negotiating the purchase price down, and then following up with improvements that add value to the property, you might find that the property's valuation can increase quite a bit in a relatively short time. That, too, builds equity you can leverage.

When Not to Maximize Your Capital

Now, having given you many different ways to maximize your capital, let me also give you a few reasons why you wouldn't want to do it.

You want to stretch yourself because that's how you grow. It's true in your intellectual life and your personal life, and it's true in your financial life as well. But there is a downside: the bigger your investment, the more peculiarities you may find—in the building itself, in the tenants, and even in the sellers and brokers.

For instance, let's start with the roof. In most single-family homes, the roof is pitched, but the bigger the apartment house, the more likely it is to have a flat roof. This can cause all kinds of problems, not least of which come from the stuff people put on the flat roof. It may have been built to include air-conditioning units and exposed pipes; there's more engineering involved in designing and building a larger place. Plus, the bigger the building, the more rooftop there is to maintain and replace when needed. In many ways, larger buildings may not have been constructed the way you would want, whether that's safety features or ease of maintaining. You really have to dig in and make sure the building is right for you.

The bigger the outside, the more stuff you'll find on the inside as well. First of all, there'll be more hallways. How well laid-out is it? Again, just because someone built it doesn't mean they designed it well. It doesn't mean they cared. Hallways need to be maintained and cleaned, and they also eat away at available living space. How do people take out the trash? Are there chutes? Where's the laundry room? Is it right next to a unit? And, if so, how loud is it? Will it make that unit unrentable? You have to make an analysis not just on the property, but also on the individual units. Is it a walk-up or is there an elevator? How narrow are those stairs? What kind of shape is that elevator in? You can see how the bigger the building, the more your problems expand.

This is true with tenants as well. The more renters you have, the more chance there is that one of them will be a bad actor. Or someone who is simply litigious. We live in a litigious world; I've been sued plenty of times. Sometimes there's poor communication between you and your tenants—maybe the paperwork hasn't been thorough enough, maybe there's a misunderstanding between you.

Even writing this book, I have been careful to say more than once that following my advice is no guarantee of success. Owning and managing properties has worked very well for me over the decades, and part of the legacy I want to leave is to pass on some of my hard-won experience to people like you. But someone will read this, sink everything they own into the first building they see, and sue me when it isn't all fun and rainbows and candies. Does it keep me from writing this? No, but it does push me to communicate as clearly as possible that the best I can do is offer you my knowledge and advice based on my own experiences, and tell you that your mileage may vary. I'll probably say that a few more times, just to drive it home.

But sometimes, you don't just get someone who misunderstands—you actually run into someone who figures, hey, you own this big building, you can afford to pay me for my troubles.

Here's a good story to illustrate my point. I once had a tenant sue me because they slipped and fell on the carpeting that was in one of my buildings. The person had hurt themselves significantly, and they sued me. Only thing is, we came to find out that they had *not* fallen on my carpet. They had fallen and hurt themselves someplace else. But unlike the owner of the place where the person really had fallen, I looked like I had deep pockets, so the tenant decided to sue me instead. The truth ultimately came out, but it was not a pleasant time.

The thing is, with a bigger location, the possibility of someone actually hurting themselves does increase, no matter how diligent you are. But the other thing that increases is the possibility of having some bad actors in the mix, people who are eager to take advantage of you. Owning a building does, to some extent, put a target on your back. Greed and envy are terrible things, especially in combination. I'm not trying to frighten you, just making sure you know what you're getting into.

Finally, the bigger the property, the more likely you are to be dealing with sellers and brokers who have already seen it all. They are going to be more sophisticated than you are. Not that you can't do business with them, but why put yourself into a position where you'll be seen as naive? A new kid who doesn't yet know their way around the block? You can counter that by projecting confidence and by asking a lot of questions, which I always did; I wanted to know everything about the property and was always asking every question I could think of. But I don't recommend it as your first go-round. The fundamentals for every property will always be the same, but there are so many more things to take into account when you're looking at twenty or thirty units or more. Until you've done it a few times, you won't necessarily know all the places to look for problems or for opportunities.

So what am I saying here? Am I telling you to play small? Absolutely not. Going big is how you build generational wealth. I'm just telling you to be smart about it. Learn on something smaller, maybe an eight-unit building. Don't go straight from a single-family home or a duplex to a twenty-unit building. Allow yourself the grace to learn as you go. You have time. Make your mistakes and learn the ropes on properties you can grow with, rather than leapfrogging over them and assuming you'll never make a mistake. That's arrogance, not confidence. How you develop real confidence is in making mistakes, fixing them, and learning how not to make them again. Don't start too small, but don't jump into the middle of the ocean, either, before you've had a swimming lesson.

In practical terms, this means stretch yourself, because no matter where you are in life, you can always achieve more by reaching for something a little bigger. But stretching does not mean breaking. There are limitations: you don't want to be so heavily in debt that you can't carry the property during hard times. You don't want to have more units than would be in demand in this particular neighborhood at that particular price point. This is research to be done and there are hard numbers to look at. It is worth doing an analysis where you anticipate the absolute worst just to see what options you might have if, in fact, the worst comes true. Being spread too thin is a dangerous place to be.

You Are Surrounded by Money

I really want you to change your mind-set about money. I said earlier that we are swimming in it. Truly, we are. You are surrounded by money and by opportunities to create money for yourself and for others. The key is to always look for a win-win.

Let me give you a couple of examples. One started with me going to a local bowling alley. I didn't go too often, but whenever I did, I always saw the same guy there. He was also Italian American, and one day we started talking. Turns out he was a real estate broker. He said he had a restaurant for sale—would I be interested in buying it? It just so happened that I had a dear friend who was a restauranteur. He told me about the restaurant and added that one of the partners was willing to stay, but they needed someone else to make up the difference in the price.

I went to my friend and set him up with the broker and the other partner. I went over all the paperwork with him, I helped put the deal together, and they offered me in on the deal with 5 percent ownership, or about $15,000. But as we got closer, they realized they didn't actually want me to be part owner of the restaurant—and that was fine, I didn't want to own part of the restaurant. (Do you know the failure rate for restaurants? Not the kind of risk I like to take.) I looked around for a win-win, and I realized that 5 percent of the business was equivalent, in terms of money ($15,000), to a 30 percent interest in just the land the restaurant sat on. I offered that to them instead: to put me on the title of the real estate as owning 30 percent of the land, but I would own nothing of the restaurant business. This solution suited everyone—in fact, they thought they had the better of the deal—so that's what we did.

I would probably have moved on because I had no interest in the restaurant business, but a couple of things happened. They had to fire their manager, and I was not yet running apartment houses full time, so I ended up managing the restaurant for them. I worked from early in the morning until late at night; it was brutal. I never saw my kids. The restaurant was a success, but I owned part of the land, not the business. I wasn't getting a piece of that success. My home life was really suffering, and after about a year, I told them that was it, they had to find a new manager, which they did. I was grateful to move on.

A few months went by, and they let me know they wanted to buy me out completely. But here's the thing: they wanted to buy me out for the same monetary amount that 5 percent had been worth when they made the deal, or $15,000. But that's not how it works. The business had increased in value (partially due to my efforts), and the land had vastly increased in value. I was on the deed, not for $15,000, but for 30 percent. At that point in time, 30 percent of the land was worth $180,000, not $15,000. I ultimately offered to let them buy me out for almost half of that, $100,000 instead of the full $180,000. That was also a win-win.

Another time, a friend of mine reached out because the property where his daughter lived was up for sale and he thought there was an opportunity for me there, so he introduced me to the owner. There was a service station with two pumps, a repair garage with a block building, a huge lot, and, in the back, a house. The owner was retiring and wanted to sell it all for $38,000. I went to the bank and got a loan for about half of it, but I was going to need to come up with an $18,000 down payment. I went to the owner and said, "Sir, I know you're retired now and you just want to sell the property, but would you consider taking almost half of it back as a loan, and I would pay you the monthly payments?" And right away, he says, "Oh, yes, sure!" Because it was a win-win; I was able to get the $18,000 as a second trust deed on the property, and he would get the $20,000 immediately from the bank while also getting regular monthly payments from me that he could count on for the next ten years.

What this meant was that I was paying both the bank and the seller from the money I earned renting out the property, so I had to get creative about how I was going to make money. It was a huge lot with a ton of potential. Since my friend George had tipped me off on the property and made the personal introductions, I offered to share ownership with him. Any money in or out, we would split 50/50—we were a partnership. He was all-in!

We improved the house on the back lot and turned it into a duplex; George's daughter stayed in the top of the house, and we rented out the bottom unit. We realized pretty quickly that the gas station barely paid for itself, so we took that down. The guy with the repair shop wanted to expand to offer a lubrication station, so we developed that. We brought in another guy who sold tires, so we had two separate business tenants. The huge lot in the back, we rented out to guys who needed a place to park their trucks. With so many streams of income, we were able to pay everyone (both the seller and the bank) off in ten years to own the property free and clear. We ultimately sold the property for $350,000—property we had bought with no money down.

We are all surrounded by money. You don't need money as much as you need business acumen, the ability to read contracts, a willingness to look for the win-win, and a readiness to jump at the opportunities that present themselves.

One last story to prove my point: there was the time someone gave me an apartment complex for no money at all. I'm not kidding. Here's the story.

CASE STUDY

Management Makes All the Difference

A friend of mine worked for the Internal Revenue Service at the same time I did, leaving to become an attorney. The firm he joined had many successful Hollywood clients, and over the years, he hired me to analyze business investments for several of them. I had great respect for his knowledge of the law, and he came to respect my business savvy, especially when it came to real estate investments.

One of his clients owned an apartment house; to say they were unhappy about it would be an understatement. The complex lost money every single month, money they would have to make up from their other income. The client was ready to get rid of the apartment. Unfortunately, because it was hemorrhaging money, they had been unable to find a buyer.

My friend asked me to take over the property. I didn't have enough money to buy it, and frankly I didn't have any interest in it. It was a nice property, but a 45-minute drive, and I knew that for the first several months at least, I would be there all the time. I told him I was sorry, I couldn't make an offer on it. My friend said no, he didn't want me to buy it. His client wanted to *give* me the property. They saw it as a money pit and just wanted it taken off their hands. They asked me to take ownership at no cost to me. I agreed on the condition that I would be given title with no legal fees and no down payment, all bills would be current as of the day I assumed ownership, and notices would go out to the property management company, the resident manager, and all tenants that I was the new owner.

The first thing I did was take point. I realized the property management company was charging 5 percent on all rent collected, but they never visited the property and weren't taking responsibility for qualifying the applications to rent. They were basically renting to anyone who walked in the door without first making sure they could afford the rent. When I asked them how often they visited the property, I was told they never came by because "the property runs itself." No property runs itself! This was a no-brainer. They were fired according to their contract requiring "due diligence." My team took over the administration and bookkeeping.

The second thing I did was replace the manager. I realize this can be a difficult step to take, but trying to retrain someone who has been doing it their way to now do it your way is fraught with difficulties. In this case, the person had also clearly not been able to handle the responsibilities. In addition, I found that the manager and his wife were overcharging for repainting vacant apartments. They left in the second month, and I replaced them with my trained manager. All the paperwork changed to reflect our requirements, which meant new rental agreements and applications moving forward.

By the third month, I had equalized the tenant rent schedules so that all tenants paid according to unit size and amenities. At the same time, we had also taken care of all repairs and service issues. Tenants realized the new management team was going to listen to their issues and be on top of their needs. We lost some tenants, but the ones we gained in their place were a better fit for the building.

Within a few months, we had turned the property around. The only problem for us was that it was far from our other properties; we (my team and I, and our repair and maintenance crews) had to travel too far to watch over the property. We decided with the positive equity we had created that we would put it on the market. From the sale, we were able to have enough trading power to buy a building much closer to us.

I share this experience with you for two reasons. First, this is another good reminder that opportunity is everywhere. This was a win for the former owner, who was no longer propping up the investment with his other income month after month, and a win for me, who got to take on a property with nothing out of pocket. If you can create a win-win situation, anything is possible.

The second reason I share this story is because it shows how you cannot forsake good management. Any business requires attention with competent, honest management; running an apartment house is no different. If it isn't for you, there's no shame in that, but don't think you can just plunk down money and let it, in the words of the fired management company, "run itself." If it's not a responsibility you are willing to take on, one you will enjoy, don't do it. My friend's very successful Hollywood client did not have any interest in his apartment house, and that's okay. We all have different inclinations and abilities, and owning

> an apartment complex wasn't right for him. Make sure
> before you invest that it's right for you.

Land Value vs. Building Value

Initially, there is a relationship between the value of the land a building sits on and the building itself. In other words, we presume that the construction of the house or the apartment complex is in proportion to the value of the land. Once upon a time, land made up about one-third to one-quarter of value of the property as a whole. And in some places, I'm sure it still does, but the Los Angeles area is not one of those places. Land here has skyrocketed in value. This has worked out well for me on occasion, but largely is irrelevant to my day-to-day. I'm not telling you to ignore the land's value, but I am telling you it's more complicated than it looks. I'll go into more detail about determining the value of the building versus the land when I talk about depreciation.

Back to the land. For all you might like to have a lot of land, you have to look at it as a resource you have to maximize to make it worth the added cost in property taxes. On your taxes, for instance, you can write off the depreciation of a building, but you can't write off the land. If the land is not a resource you plan to use, it's a waste of your money.

You need enough land for there to be sufficient parking, for instance. That's one of the key factors you should consider whenever you look at a property. A lack of parking is a clear reason for me to pass on a property. But other than that, how much land do you really need? It all depends on what your intentions are.

A typical situation you hear about all the time is where someone has a huge lot with only one house on it, and there's a buyer who wants the lot in order to build a high-rise. They see future value, in terms of an income property with multiple units, for the land. But a lot of things can go wrong between now and that future value. For one thing, you have to make sure not just that the neighborhood is able to sustain that much additional housing now, but that it will continue to do so in the future. Neighborhoods change. One thing that can sink a neighborhood is when developers rush to build residential units, but there's no additional infrastructure put in place, like schools or public transportation. Local schools can become overcrowded as a wave of new tenants floods in, and that can negatively impact how the schools are perceived, and in fact how well they function. The neighborhood can change for other reasons as well, so that by the time you have finished building this fifty-unit high-rise, the demand is no longer there. Remember my mother. The bigger the building, the more risk you assume.

Also, property tax is based on both land and building, and no one is more experienced at appraising than the tax appraisers. They know exactly what everything goes for in your area; you don't want to be out of sync. You have to be able to justify, as a businessperson, both your purchase price and the property taxes on a property. How will it make sense to you as a business investment? The bottom line is, if you're not going to either improve the empty land by building more units to increase your income or sell it to someone else so that they can improve it, you are wasting your money and your time. This is an income property, not your home. You have to be dispassionate and make sure you are using every resource wisely.

Insurance

Insurance is not optional. First of all, the lender—usually the bank when you have a mortgage—will always require insurance, both a fire policy and a liability policy, and depending on where you are, other policies that are necessary to protect their investment. Most insurance brokers evaluate the coverage based on the purchase price of the building (as opposed to the price of the land). The lender will not give you a loan without insurance, so there's no point in arguing it. Besides, it's perfectly appropriate; you want your investment protected. It's for your own good as much as it is for theirs. The lender will want to see that you're covered for at least what you borrowed, but you want to cover more than that. You also want to have life insurance. The very last thing you want is for your family to be wiped out financially if something happens to you. I carried enough life insurance to pay off all of our debt if something had happened to me. It's the right thing to do.

CASE STUDY

The Importance of Insurance

You have to build insurance into your budget from the beginning; it is simply too important to cut corners. Let me illustrate with an example of one time when insurance was critically important to me.

During the Los Angeles riots, the apartment complex next to the one I owned was very badly damaged. The owner decided not to try to build back and instead walked away, turning the property over to the bank. The bank employed a contractor to restore the property, hoping possibly that he would want to buy it himself, but the contractor was in high demand fixing up a huge portfolio of properties. He was satisfied to have made his money in the restoration; the last thing he wanted to do was manage property. The bank, meanwhile, very much wanted to get the property off its bankruptcy list.

I got to know the contractor while he was working on the building, and when he was done, he suggested I approach the bank to buy the property. It only took one visit. I gave the bank my property history and financial statement; then and there, they decided to give me the loan and title, with no down payment.

Sadly, within several months, someone firebombed the building. It was a total loss, and the remains were demolished. But insurance is a nonnegotiable line item to me. From the moment I took ownership, I kept the building fully insured. The bank collected the insurance, which covered the loan, and let me have the empty lot. Later, when the land had appreciated, I sold the lot and used the proceeds to buy another building.

I offer this as a stark example of the importance of insurance. You can't anticipate every outcome, and insurance is an important defense against misfortune. But this is also an example of the importance of making connections. You never know where an opportunity will come from. You have to get to know people and let them get to know you. That's how deals get made.

Finally, one word of warning: while the apartment house policies are relatively generic, I would only want to deal with insurance brokers who are familiar with apartment buildings. As with everything, an expert will save you time and headaches in the long run. Get someone who knows what they're doing.

CHAPTER SEVEN

DEVELOPING RELATIONSHIPS

This is a business of relationships. You have to develop a good relationship with your own broker, but also with the seller's broker. You need to develop a good relationship with your tenants, with your employees, with the people you hire to maintain the grounds. It's a partnership involving everyone.

How do you develop good relationships? First off, you need to keep your word. I can't stress this enough. Do not default on your loans. Show up when you say you will. Be someone they can trust, and you will earn the benefit of that trust.

Here's an example. I needed a loan for a property I wanted to buy. I was getting a good deal on it and there was a reason for that: no one had been able to make a go of it. The area had a bad reputation, and my banker was a little nervous. He called me at home over the weekend to talk about it. "Robert, are you sure?" he asked. "The neighborhood has a lot of foreclosures. I don't think you'll be able to make a go of it." But I was sure. I knew the area he was describing was near the property I wanted, but it was on the cusp of a neighborhood that was picking up. The property itself had been neglected and there was a lot of room for improvement—just the kind of situation I liked. I told him not to worry, his investment was safe. And here's the thing: he believed me. I got the loan. He believed me because I had never lied to him. I had never defaulted. It had taken years to build up that level of trust, and it happened, not by accident, but by being someone others could count on. Don't squander that kind of personal capital or it won't be there when you really need it.

You also need to get comfortable talking to people. It may be that it's easier for you to talk to some kinds of people than to others; that's certainly true for me. I've always looked for neighborhoods where I felt comfortable. These aren't necessarily the ritziest neighborhoods! I'll leave those for the friend I mentioned earlier. I've worked all my life and I like to be around working people. Your property has to suit your style.

Here's some homework for you. Go look at some neighborhoods that have apartment buildings. They don't even have to be buildings on the market yet; I've often scouted out neighborhoods I wanted to be in long before the place I ended up buying was available. Drive around to get a sense of what's available in that area, then park and get out and walk. Go back to that Street Appeal Survey I gave you in the Appraising a Property chapter and fill it out. Talk to some people who live in the area. What do they like about their apartment? What do they wish were different? Do they feel the neighborhood is improving or going downhill? Go to each neighborhood twice, once on a weekday and once on a weekend; maybe even swing by at night. Visit at least five different neighborhoods to get a sense of the people as well as the places. (Take your time, this book isn't going anywhere . . . .)

Also, this has to be said: the worst mistake you can make is to put an offer on the first property you see. You can't be in that much of a hurry; there is so much you don't know, you don't understand. Just getting out there and visiting multiple locations will open your eyes to how widely properties differ, how many things you need to account for. It will, I hope, encourage you to push yourself to learn more before you jump into a deal.

Did you do it? Did you visit a few different neighborhoods and get a real feel for the areas? Great! For some people, just having to talk to a single tenant or even visit and evaluate more than one property has them close this book forever. These are not people who would have enjoyed owning and managing property, and that's fine. We all have different strengths. If you don't like people, this may not be the business for you.

But if you do like people and found yourself excited by what you learned on your field trips, terrific! I'm guessing you'll have started to notice things you never really thought of before. Things like how quiet or how lively a neighborhood might be, and how much that can change on a weekday versus a weekend. Nuances between the cultures of different neighborhoods, their socioeconomic makeup, whether they cater to young families or to urban professionals or to a melting pot of generations and backgrounds. Where did you feel the most comfortable? Where would you want to live? That was always a consideration for me: Could I see myself living here? Could I raise a family here? You want to focus on neighborhoods where the answer is a strong *yes*.

Why am I talking about people? Because, unlike a widget factory, an apartment complex deals in human beings in all their complicated glory. Of course, this is a business and you are in it to make money, but it's a business that involves people at their most vulnerable, in their homes. You can't divorce people from the business of providing shelter. I truly believe this is a partnership between you and your tenants. They have a need for a home, which you are providing in exchange for money. The relationship should be mutually beneficial and mutually respectful.

Get Your Own House in Order

I've mentioned a couple of times already that real estate is a business of relationships. Let me go a little deeper here to talk about some important relationships that might not be on your radar: those with your partners and your family.

We tend to take these relationships for granted. That is a mistake.

I'm not talking about how important these relationships are for a life worth living. I believe, as a businessman, that it is critical to make sure there is clear communication, understanding, and fairness in our relationships with family and any financial partners (some of whom may also be family) for the well-being of our business.

Here's the brutal truth: different expectations regarding responsibilities, decision-making authority, and potential financial rewards can undermine or even end any relationship. Owning something together, especially something as demanding and complex as a multiple-unit apartment house, is a kind of marriage where each party is bound to the other. A dysfunctional relationship can destroy your bonds to each other as well as any possibility of making a success of your business.

How many sellers out there are partners who have soured on each other or marriages that have ended in divorce? The pressure of co-ownership may not have been the nail in the coffin, but it sure helped dig the grave.

So how do you prevent that? Clear and respectful communication is a great place to start.

Before you put an offer on anything, you need to sit down with each of your partners separately and with all of them together to discuss, understand, and clarify everyone's position. Your partners include your spouse or significant other; in fact, that should be your first conversation. Remember that this adventure involves your joint savings, which is scary enough, but also your time, which is the foundation of your relationship. You both need to agree on the parameters of the business; at its most basic, you need to agree on who is going to do what. Who will deal with tenant problems? Who will collect the rent? Who will tend to the grounds? Clean out the empty apartments? Repaint the walls? Sure, you might be able to hire people to help with some of it, but if you're just getting started in the business, you may need to sock every possible dollar away. At the very least, you should do your own bookkeeping so that you understand exactly how much is coming in and going out, and where it's allocated.

You need to be careful as well with this division of labor, because nothing is easily split 50/50. Some things take longer while other things are more physically taxing. These days, you're both probably working full-time jobs; if you're adding what will be at minimum another part-time job on top of that, how will that affect the division of labor at home? Nothing here is insurmountable, but it's all worth figuring out before resentments start festering.

You also need to spell out how you're going to support each other. Where do you anticipate problems? How can you preempt them, or at least put a system in place to mitigate them? What happens if one of you gets sick? Or if you have children, what happens if childcare falls through? Brainstorm all the things that may go wrong and come up with backup plans and clear areas of authority for each of you, so that one of you isn't bearing the burdens while the other one calls all the shots. One way to overcome familial resistance to your plans is to create a situation where everyone has responsibility, but everyone also reaps some benefits. It's going to be hard work and there will be scary times; if everyone doesn't feel valued, it can tear your family apart.

I saw this dynamic play out with my own parents. My mother had a tremendous capacity for risk-taking; my father, much less. My mother had grand ambitions and rarely rested, while my father worked extremely hard seasonally and then was content to lie back, listen to music, and read during his time off. Their communication skills were, well, not what I hope for you: my mother actually put our family home on the market without telling my father and used the funds to buy an apartment complex that we then had to move into. My father hated it. Although they loved each other and never divorced, they did separate, and part of the reason was that they had never been on the same team.

Build your team now, before there's so much at stake.

Once you've created a united front with your family and an equitable division of labor, you need to look at everyone else who may be partnering with you. Division of ownership is equally important and also needs to be crystal clear. Is your mom giving you a loan? Make sure you both understand the parameters. Is it to be paid back monthly with interest or is it an investment that entitles her to a percentage of the profits? You may have one thing in mind and she may have something very different. The only way to know is to sit down and hash it out, point by point.

Division of ownership can be complicated. It may seem to you that a 50/50 split is fair, especially if you're both putting in the same amount of money, but money is only part of the investment. Are you both putting the same amount of time into management, maintenance, or bookkeeping? If you are equal partners, who has final say? What happens if one of you needs money in a hurry—does that force a sale? There are a hundred things to take under consideration. Settle in for a long conversation and expect to be surprised by what each of you has taken for granted. And that's fine. Understanding each other's positions is a great place to start your negotiations. Hammer out a deal that doesn't leave resentment in its wake.

While you're talking about ownership, you should also talk about the division of profit. Nothing is written in stone, until it is, in fact, written and signed. Each of you may think your own contribution is the most important; that's to be expected. We are all the stars of our own movies. Talk it out with mutual respect and actively try to understand the other's point of view. You may decide you can't move forward because there is some insurmountable difference of opinion. Congratulations! The time to find that out is now, before you make an offer, not after you've been given the deed. More likely, however, is that you will find a middle ground you can both live with.

That united front I mentioned earlier should extend to every partner. You have to present one face to the residents, the vendors, the brokers, the lenders, and to any encounter outside the ownership. I'm not saying you'll never disagree. You're human! Of course you'll disagree. But you do it in private. You work things out between yourselves and present one consistent message to the rest of the world.

Once you have a division of power, labor, ownership, and profit that is mutually acceptable, put it in writing. Nothing in business is real if it's not in writing. That is possibly the best advice I will ever give you, so take it to heart.

Contracts

This is probably a good place for me to say a few words about lawyers.

Look, you need contracts, that's a given. Especially if you have outside people, family or business partners, putting up some of the money for the purchase of the property, you need to have contracts with them that are separate from the actual purchase contract for the property. You need your agreements with your partners to be clear and legally enforceable. You probably need to talk to a lawyer for that. Maybe you need to set up a trust; again, that takes someone who knows what they're doing, a lawyer with experience in the field. I am not a lawyer. Everything I give you is advice from my perspective, but not to be taken as a sure thing. When it comes to the law in particular, I want you to have expertise at your fingertips. Lawyers are those experts.

That said, you need to understand contracts on your own.

You need to take responsibility for reading contracts, seeing where they might leave you vulnerable, and learning what you can ask to be added that gives you some protection. Take a class in real estate law. Read books. Lots of books. Follow people online, listen to podcasts, watch interviews and webinars. And, yes, ask lawyers to talk you through the fine print. But the buck stops with you. It's important for you to take responsibility for your business, and contracts are the language of business.

Also, lawyers can often slow things down. It's not that they don't have your best interests at heart; I hope they do. And they know the law. But they're not necessarily businesspeople. Lawyers are trained to be adversarial. That is baked into a law school education here in the United States. And you don't necessarily want to be adversarial when you are negotiating a deal. What you want to be is fair, and you want there to be guardrails in place, legally, to make sure the other people treat you fairly as well. You may need to get the advice of a lawyer to identify those guardrails, but that doesn't mean you want them in a room negotiating with you, and you certainly don't want to absorb an "us versus them" mentality—not from the lawyer or from the broker or from cultural expectations. You bringing in a lawyer can scare the other side into lawyering up themselves, and the next thing you know, the deal falls through. Making the deal should be thought of as a partnership of all involved.

There is nothing like firsthand experience when it comes to understanding contracts. Read everything yourself. If you don't understand, that's when you go to your broker or your lawyer and ask for a detailed explanation. Find a mentor, read books on real estate contracts, take classes at your local community college. I used to take night classes on real estate at my local junior college after work. I learned a little bit about everything in that class, including escrow and the real estate market. You can even study for the realtor's exam, even if you never plan to become a realtor—you will learn so much about the business by approaching it from a broker's perspective. Live in your local library; so many authors have been so generous over the years, passing on their hard-won knowledge. Finally, another benefit of starting small and not spreading yourself too thin financially is that you can learn from the school of hard knocks a little bit without too much exposure.

Purchase agreements used to be two pages long when I first started out in real estate. They are a lot longer than that now! And that's a good thing. It can make expectations clearer and help protect you both when you're a buyer and when you're a seller. But you still have to read every word. This is a legally binding agreement, so why wouldn't you make sure you understand it? Ask your broker why something is included and what it means to you. Have an inquiring mind at every step of the journey. The things you will learn will not just help you avoid disaster with this deal, but also with other deals two or three properties down the road. You are always applying the best practices you pick up along the way.

Even before you sign the contract, when you put down your deposit, make sure there's a contingency agreement with your deposit that includes an option for you to walk away. Make sure the contingency is along the lines of the following: if you find out there's something about the property that isn't satisfactory, you can retrieve your deposit and walk away from the deal with no financial penalty. The verbiage here is very much in your favor, as it's your satisfaction that has to be met. No one can argue with how satisfied you are. This contingency can cover all sorts of ills, from the condition of the units to the age of the roof. Also, your deposit doesn't go directly to the seller; it is in the broker's hands. Yet another reason to have a good relationship with both brokers.

You can't just sign a boilerplate contract and assume you're golden.

I noticed early on that even the standard agreement, mandated by state law, didn't have all the things I wanted to see in a contract. So what did I do? I added a couple of lines to make sure that I had an escape clause to get out of the deal, and similarly I always made sure there was wording to encourage them to behave appropriately right to the end.

People are people, and that means that sometimes they're going to take what they think is the easy way out, or they're going to feel entitled to everything that isn't tied down. I remember one time when the escrow was sixty days and the seller decided, hey, it's not my building anymore, I don't have to cut the grass. He let his groundskeepers go and the place went to seed before I took ownership. Obviously, this was not okay. It depresses the street appeal and tenants might even think the new owner (me!) was too cheap to cut the grass, which could lead them to look for a new place to live. The last thing I want is a mass exodus of tenants just as I take possession. That building is the seller's responsibility until the day escrow closes and I take the keys. I've had to send letters informing the seller that they had neglected the property; I've even had to take people to court just to make sure they do the decent thing and reimburse me for the cost of repairing the mess they created. I've even had some sellers who replaced fixtures in the lobby with cheaper ones so they could take the nice ones with them. No, no, no. All of those things are part of the sale. Unfortunately, some people will take anything that's not nailed down on their way out.

That's another reason for you to be honorable: you'll stand out in the crowd. People will remember you and want to work with you again. I have a couple of brokers who would be on the lookout for the kind of property I'd want. "Robert," they'd call to say, "I have a property that I know you're going to buy." And they'd be right! They didn't call me for every property, but for ones that they knew would suit me, I was their first and sometimes only call. Having people who want to work with you can save you a lot of time and energy because they will be looking out for properties on your behalf, just to have the chance to work with you again.

You also want to think about what you can do for other people. This is a sorely neglected part of networking. It's not that it's a quid pro quo relationship—you are not helping them with the expectation that they owe you. You are instead helping them because their success is your success. When your friends and colleagues do well, that is a reason to celebrate, just because you want to see good people succeed. But it also means that they are in an even better position to help you down the line. I have a friend who says, "Circles rise together," and that is true in real estate as in life.

What kind of favors are we talking about? Again, not the kind of favors that you "call in." Just general helping out. For instance, I mentioned that a couple of realtors I've worked with on several occasions started keeping an eye out for buildings that fit my vision. I'd like to think I was their first call when they found one. Those same realtors would also sometimes call me and say, "Robert, I have a property and I'm going to be honest with you, I don't think it's right for you. But I would appreciate it if you'd come out and take a look." And I always would. Why? Because I knew it helped them look good to their client that they could get potential buyers to show up and check out the property quickly.

This is the best kind of favor to do because so much good comes out of it: I help them out and strengthen our relationship while at the same time getting a look at a new property on the market. It's possible they were wrong, and I might be the right buyer after all; it's a lot more likely that I might know the right buyer and steer them in that direction. Creating connection between people you know whenever possible is always a win. When it works out, you're a hero to both parties! Even if it doesn't work out, people know you tried.

When Relationships Change

I would be remiss if I didn't warn you that some of your relationships won't withstand your success. Hopefully, when you look at owning an apartment house, you see it as an opportunity to expand your skills, invest in your future, and provide homes for tenants who need them. You recognize that there's an element of risk and a lot of hard work ahead of you.

Some of your family and friends, however, may see it as you flaunting your wealth.

I don't know what to tell you other than it's really not about you. I have lost friends and I have seen others go through difficulties with family members over the difference in status that they perceive in the owning of an investment property. But it's their perception, not your reality, that is at fault. Don't take it personally. If you can salvage the relationship, I wish you well, but I will say that true friends and loved ones aren't jealous when you succeed. Instead, they will relish your growth, your happiness, and your new adventure. Those who don't, well, perhaps it's best to let them go.

CASE STUDY

The Golden Deal

Several years ago, my ultimate goal was within sight: I had always planned to acquire apartment houses until I reached my five-hundred-unit goal. A friend of mine, one of the brokers I worked with regularly, called to let me know of a property that would help me reach that goal and, in fact, slightly surpass it. The available property was coming up at an estate sale, neglected and poorly marketed. It did, however, meet all of the parameters I was looking for: neighborhood, land for street upgrade, solid construction, and tremendous opportunity for upgrades. In addition, it was located within the circle of properties we already owned. This is why you want to develop a good relationship with everyone you work with whenever possible: my friend was always keeping an eye out for the kind of property that would be a good fit for me, and this one was ideal. The property had been owned for fifteen or twenty years by a fellow who decided he wanted to rent rooms

---

to graduate students at a local seminary. Students were a good fit for him because he never had to do any maintenance in exchange for keeping the rent low.

His target audience wasn't families or anyone who was trying to build a home there, but rather students who were only going to be there a couple of years before moving on; all they cared about was low rent. Over the years, he made some good income, took the depreciation, and never had to put much effort into it. It worked for him, but it meant the property had been sorely neglected by the time he passed away. It went to his heirs and ultimately they had to go through the courts to enact the sale.

I went ahead and made an offer ahead of the court date. Mine was the first offer on the property, so I bid within the legal allowance of 15 percent under the asking price (your situation may vary depending on the state you live in). What this meant was that anyone else bidding was now required to bid at least the original asking price. The trustee of the property had listed it at an asking price less than what the property was actually worth—it may seem counterintuitive, but this worked in the trust's favor so they would pay less estate tax. There's always a range available to you for appraising the property; they chose the low end of the range, and that was great for me because I'd be getting a bargain. But there was a catch: the money had to be available to pay out the property. In other words, the buyer had to have the entire amount for the purchase in hand almost immediately—the first 25 percent was due at the close of the final bid, and the rest (75 percent) within twenty-four hours. This is a big deal; you don't just need a down payment, you need it all.

I had three weeks before the court date. I sold some of my stock portfolio to cover the down payment, and I actually had that money on me, the entire down payment, in my pocket as a money order. I ran around, used all my connections, and finally found a banker who gave me the assurance that I could have a loan covering the rest of the money immediately upon winning the property. I had one more very important safeguard: my broker. I said, "If you're really a friend, you'll keep me from getting sucked into a bidding war." He promised to hold me back. I told him what my highest bid would be, and I felt better having that safeguard in place. Because I'm human, just like everyone else. I like to win!

This is probably a good time to mention that I don't recommend estate sales. People prey on property auctions to get the best possible deals, but not all auctions are aboveboard. And buyers tend to go a little crazy; everyone gets carried away. You end up taking things personally, as if you were in a battle with the other bidders. That kind of energy works against you—you end up spending too much money or buying a property that's not truly the best fit for you. You'll see in a minute, even I didn't come out of this one unscathed! So even though I'm telling you this story, this is more of a cautionary tale than a recommendation for you to seek out an estate sale.

Back to my auction. On the day of the sale, there was a whole crowd at the courthouse. It was electrifying, filled with both lookie-loos and various serious bidders who wanted the opportunity to own the property. I was sworn in, asked by the judge if I had made the bid, if I had the cash on hand for the down payment.

Yes and yes. So far, things were going as planned. The judge then asked if there were any other bidders, and one person popped up, bidding the full asking price. My heart sank. There went my great deal! Sure enough, other bidders jumped in, and the next thing you know, we got into a bidding war. As they upped their offers, I increased my bid to meet the new challengers. My broker did his best, reminding me when I hit my upper limit that I didn't want to keep at it. The building might still have been perfect for me, but it was no longer a good deal. I decided to go one bid beyond that limit, but once again, I was outbid. This time, I was done. I walked away.

But this is not the end of the story.

The woman who won the bidding war didn't actually have the money order for the down payment. I don't know how the court let her out of there without paying it, but maybe they didn't want to go through another bidding war. In any case, they gave her a few days. However, as it turned out, not only did she not have the down payment, but she didn't have the loan for the full amount in place either.

What does she do? She calls me.

She asks me where I was able to get my loan to cover the property.

Now, let's be clear. This took a lot of nerve on her part. She drives up the price, outbids me, and then wants me to tell her where to get the loan for it? What gall! But I try not to burn a bridge if I can avoid it, so I told her the name of the bank where I was going to get my financing. She thanked me and hung up. I heard from her again a few days later. Turns out, she was unable to get the loan anywhere. She asked me if I would be willing to buy the property from her for the same amount she had bid on it. And I did.

This is why you don't hold grudges and you don't burn bridges.

If I had slammed the phone down on her when she called to ask me where I'd gotten my loan, I would never have been given the opportunity to buy the property. And it was still a great deal for me, a win-win. Even though I ended up paying a little more than I wanted, within a space of a few months I had raised the property value. I started by hiring a new manager whom I trained, landscaping the grounds, providing more parking spaces, and painting the exterior. Within two years, I had remodeled all the units. With all these upgrades, the property value increased by 25 percent over my purchase price, while the cost of the upgrades themselves were paid off in three years.

This was my final purchase. My final acquisitions goal was met. I had just over five hundred units, all within an area that made it easy for my team to clean, maintain, landscape, and manage the properties on an ongoing basis. All that I had worked for to have a smooth apartment house management operation was in place.

Sadly, this became my final purchase for another reason: my beloved first wife, Bernice, passed away soon after this deal. The joy of acquisition went out of it for me. We'd had many difficult years, although the thrill of building our financial future together had always kept us going. I was grateful for everyone who had helped us along the way, and ultimately, I was ready to move on to new challenges, having the assurance of a well-run business, steady income, and sufficient funds for philanthropy. This was true financial freedom, and I wish it for all of you reading this.

PART THREE
MANAGEMENT

Chapter Eight

Why Managing Is the Secret Sauce

Congratulations! You have decided to buy an apartment complex and perhaps have even figured out your finances, your preferred neighborhood, and your plan to recoup your investment. But wait! Don't sign on the dotted line quite yet. Before you decide you're ready to be an owner, you should understand what goes into managing a building once you have one.

Absentee Landlords

Landlords have often been given a bad reputation in American culture. Greedy, pitiless owners of unsafe, even uninhabitable apartments—that is often how they are portrayed. As a landlord who has always worked to make sure my tenants live in the best possible conditions, I take offense at those portrayals.

But what I really take offense at are the people who live up to the stereotype.

You cannot simply buy a building and rest on your laurels. There are owners who buy the building and then do nothing more themselves, take on no personal responsibility to make sure the units are worth living in. These people tend to buy apartment houses and other real estate because of the advantageous tax write-offs, and maybe a little bit out of pride of ownership. But pride of ownership can't stop at writing the check; you're not hoarding buildings, you're developing them. It takes effort.

Over the years, I've been a consultant for many people who were looking to buy an apartment house, and I hope I've always given them good advice. I remember two, however, both in high-income professions, who were both just looking for the tax deduction. They both bought properties that needed some improvement, but improving them, making them into places that people would want to live in, was not part of their plan. They weren't trying to build something from their investment, and I guess there are those kinds of people in the world as well, but you don't have to be one of them.

Those who don't want to put in the effort themselves often hire managers or management companies to deal with the day-to-day. I'm not saying you have to do everything yourself; realistically, there's no way you can mow every lawn and paint every wall, although my family and I have all done a lot of mowing and painting in our day. But there's a difference between hiring people to help you manage your buildings and abdicating all responsibility for management to people who have no stake in the building's success. And I'm not just talking about an anonymous company run by strangers. Even worse, in my opinion, is when you hire a relative to run the building for you. What incentive do they have to create the kind of place tenants will want to keep living in and even recommend to their friends? You may feel like you're doing them a favor by giving them a job; they may feel like they're doing you a favor by taking over a job you don't want to do.

Favors are not a good way to run a business! Your cousin's spouse probably has no desire to be in management, much less the skills required. And you may not want to rock the boat with family, meaning you can't give appropriate feedback, much less fire them. There is no way this situation will turn out well for your tenants, for your financial success, or for you personally.

Having said that, I do make one exception to not hiring family members as managers, and that is for family members you intend to someday take over the business. Usually, your children. All of my kids were at some point given a building to manage, but not in a vacuum and not because I didn't want to be bothered. It was part of the training because I knew someday they would be taking over for me. There's a difference between bringing on a manager in order to give them life experience, training, and a better understanding of the business, and bringing on a manager so you can just dump the problems in their lap and walk away. And the biggest difference is the stake that person has in learning everything they can and working to improve. The greatest gift you can give your kids is to instill in them the same pride of owner-ship that (I hope) is in you. And it's also a great gift for your tenants to be managed by someone who has a reason to care.

The bottom line is if you're just going to buy a property and hand over all the decision-making to someone else while you move on to the next investment, you are setting yourself up to become not a land-lord, but a slumlord. Not only is this a terrible investment in your community, it is also a terrible investment in your future. Creating a better experience for tenants isn't just better for them—it is better for your bottom line. Being directly involved in the management of your building brings you additional earnings from settled tenants who keep your vacancy rates low and may even refer friends to you when a unit does open. It allows you to charge at the top of the market, maximizing your rate of return on investment. It also gives you a sense of pride to be providing excellent shelter to those who need it. There is a connec-tion between you and your tenants; you each depend upon the other for the best possible outcome. While all of this is better for you finan-cially, the greatest payoff to me is the satisfaction of being in charge of my own investment. I'm not one to leave decision-making to others, and it's a stance that has served me well.

Being a hands-on owner also protects your investment by mini-mizing the risk of someone else letting the facilities go to ruin or renting to the wrong people. I have a friend who bought a summer house in Maine, even though he lived in Virginia, and had a management company rent it out for most of the year. The management company just wanted to keep it occupied; they didn't really care who was in it. Partiers routinely trashed the place, several people stole furnishings when they left, and it ultimately burned down in an accidental fire. You can't always determine at the moment if the people you are renting to are honorable or not, but if you're personally involved, you can tell over time what kind of tenant they are. And then you can take appropriate and legal steps to minimize the damage to your unit and the reputation of your building.

Your Team

There will be many people on your team (more on that below), but I want to review the key players and their important roles.

The Owner

First and foremost, there is you. Ultimately, everything is your responsibility. You will hire people to take care of various scopes of work, but you need to hire people who are competent and who will keep you informed. All decisions end with you. This is not only a level of responsibility but also a level of leadership that some people are not willing to take on. If that's you, that's fine; better to know now than after you've bought a property.

Paperwork is a big part of the job description. It is up to you to review all contracts, local ordinances, insurance coverage, rental agreements, and applications from potential tenants. You will also need to receive multiple bids on any maintenance work and review them. Don't just go for the cheapest one! You often get what you pay for, and sometimes what looks like the cheaper option on paper turns out to cost you a lot more, either because the scope of the work is not on par with other bids, or the experience level of the workers is lacking. Eventually, you will find people you trust, but there is great value to getting multiple bids for everything as you get started. Just like looking at multiple properties, it's only when you compare directly to other companies that you can see what your available options are, and which matter most to you. Plus, it will give you experience reading bids and contracts that will pay off later when you need to be able to distinguish between vendors on a major, expensive project. Get that experience as soon as you can on projects where the stakes are lower.

There are also your own business practices to consider. Some of it is obvious: you'll need to set up bank accounts so you can deposit the rent checks. Some is a bit more complicated: you'll need to create an accounting system so that you know exactly what is coming in, what is going out, and what is being set aside for emergencies and recurring needed upgrades, such new water heaters, roof repairs, and other improvements. You might want to take advantage, for instance, of new energy-efficient lights or laundry machines, and while these may have a positive impact on your electricity bills over a number of years, they still require an upfront investment to reap that benefit. Really, you need to do for your building what you probably need to do for your life: set up a realistic budget that includes income, outgo, and money set aside for the payment of taxes as well as for emergencies. In your personal life, you may have let this slide, but with a business, "letting it slide" or "winging it" is not an option. You need to understand and account for every expense and every rent payment. It will also make it easier to do your taxes and it will become critical should you be audited down the road.

I can't stress enough how important a complete and accurate accounting system is. You can hire an expert to help you set it up, and you might even have an administrative assistant to help you keep the books, but going over them yourself on a regular basis is part of your job as owner. The ongoing analysis of your income and expenses can help you make the best possible decisions for your future stability and help you right the ship early if things start to go awry.

The Manager

You may operate as the owner/manager, especially for your first building. In fact, I recommend it because you will learn so much about the business. It will help you make better decisions down the line in terms of what apartment houses you want to acquire. It will also help you find the right people to be managers for subsequent buildings and when you no longer have the time or desire to manage directly, because you will know exactly what the job entails and what skill sets are needed.

The most important asset I look for is attitude. You can't put someone in this position who only wants to cut corners, for instance, or who treats your tenants with disdain. You need someone who is a professional in all ways, from how they interact with others to how they present themselves to their personal integrity and desire to be part of your team. You need someone who can troubleshoot a wide variety of issues and can interact with the tenants with a positive attitude and a great deal of tact.

Above all, you need someone who can communicate well. Your manager is your eyes and ears on the ground. They are on the front lines of any problem or dispute or crisis; they need to be level-headed, fair, and able to explain the situation to you with full context. They need to care. Having a bad manager can undermine everything you're trying to do to build your building's reputation as a top-notch place to live, and that in turn will have an impact on your financial stability. Problems only grow bigger when ignored, and people also don't want to live in a place where their concerns are dismissed or they feel under-valued. A good manager handles problems when they are still small and more easily (and inexpensively) fixed, and makes tenants feel appreciated and at home. They are an investment in your future.

Administration

Your management team may consist of a manager and several assistants, or it may just be you alone at the beginning. No matter what, you need a can-do attitude. You also need a lot of forms! Forms and checklists are a way to standardize communication with tenants so that you treat everyone fairly. They also prevent you from forgetting to document important issues, such as the condition of the unit when someone moved in—which is going to matter quite a lot when they move out.

Here are some of the forms you will need:

- A move-in form that documents the condition of the unit before a tenant moves in
- A move-out form; essentially, the same document as above, only it is filled out when a tenant moves out
- Rental agreements. These are contracts and legally binding; make sure they are clear and follow all local laws. This is one of the times when getting the advice of a lawyer who specializes in this field is a good idea.
- Repair request forms
- Other notices, such as one to give notice before you have to enter the unit for whatever reason, or a notice of a lease violation. If they need to fill out forms in order to, say, book the community room for a party, you will want to have those forms on hand as well. Forms are an excellent way to provide structure within predictable communications, not to mention that they help you keep track of what's going on within your community.

It is incredibly important that everyone (management and tenants alike) understands the steps that are taken for any interaction. You should have clear, written guidelines for what represents a violation of the lease agreement, for instance, and also what the next steps are, from notice to warning to eviction proceedings. By the same token, it should be made clear what happens when someone submits a repair request. How long will it take to get it fixed? Will they receive notice before someone comes in to do the repairs? Will that person be supervised while they are in their house if, for instance, the owner is not at home? These are all questions that tenants may reasonably have, so spell it out in writing for them. People feel safe when they know what happens next; it takes any problem down a notch. It also means your management team doesn't have to spend all their time answering the same five questions.

Finally, you will need paperwork to make expectations clear for your own employees. Timecards, forms to requisition office supplies, and even a schedule of rental receipts and a way to keep track of who has paid what rent and when—all of these simplify the job of keeping track of income and outgo. Keeping accurate and timely records is critical to your business success. It's not just important for tax purposes; it gives you the foundation from which to make accurate financial decisions. And keeping comprehensive records of tenants—not just their rental payments, but notes on interactions, complaints, even repairs completed—will serve you well during any confrontation.

Hiring Professionals

It's not just managers or support staff you will need to hire, but also professionals who will do everything from routine maintenance to emergency repairs. The important thing is that you spend the time now to set up those relationships before you need them, rather than waiting until the roof is falling in or the pipes are leaking.

When you purchase the property, one of the things you will do is have the seller notify their vendors of the change in ownership. It is usually worth meeting with these people in advance to discuss your vision for the property, ascertain their level of expertise, and see whether or not you would be a good fit. Eventually, you will probably have people that you know you want to work with, but especially in your first few properties, it's good to meet a lot of professionals. Just like when you first started looking at real estate and you weren't yet sure what mattered to you and what didn't, so, too, when meeting professionals you begin to discern what matters in that kind of relationship. The baseline, of course, should be that they are competent, whether they are accountants or landscapers, but beyond that, what are you looking for? Do you want someone with imagination and a willingness to try new things? Or are you looking for someone to follow your directions exactly? Does it matter to you that you get along well with them, or can you handle someone who is grumpy but exceptionally good at their job? There is no right or wrong beyond what will work best for you.

I like to work with people who are smart, competent, and resourceful, and have integrity. I'm willing to help train people to grow within the organization, but I want to work with those who are willing to learn. In case you haven't figured it out by now, I was very involved in all aspects of building my family business; having someone who was difficult to work with would have cost me time I didn't have. As you work with people, you will discover what works for you.

Here is a list of all the different types of professionals I have worked with over the years in my real estate business, in no particular order:

- Accountants
- Lawyers
- Gardeners
- Landscape designers
- Painters
- Roofers
- Plumbers
- Electricians
- Handymen
- Cleaners
- Managers
- Clerical workers/administrative assistants

These professionals fall into roughly three categories: Employees, Independent Contractors, and, for want of a better term, Occasional Necessities. Here's what I mean.

Employees are, obviously, people you hire to take care of the ongoing business, things that happen every day. For instance, if you are not going to be the hands-on manager (and that's okay; it's not the managing per se that matters, it's the willingness to take on the decision-making, to have the buck stop with you), you will need a manager for each property you own. Sometimes managers live in the building, sometimes they don't. In any event, they need to be able to be contacted by tenants during regular business hours. You will also need them to handle emergencies. Having a special number for that or having the manager's number go to an answering service after hours that can alert you to true emergencies (fires, plumbing disasters, etc.) would be a solution that keeps your manager from being on duty 24/7, but also provides a direct way for tenants to let the management know when something is truly wrong. As your business grows, you might need an assistant to help you manage the calls, emails, and paperwork associated with your (I hope) many properties. These are people who work directly for you; they are on your payroll.

Independent contractors are more like that hypothetical answering service. You don't pay the individuals directly; you pay the company that provides them. This is largely how you will staff service people to do all the routine maintenance. Especially when you are just getting started, the vast majority of people you work with will be employees of other companies that you contract out to. Why? Because you won't have enough work to keep, say, a painter busy all the time. Or even a gardener, no matter how fast the grass grows. You will contract with companies that provide these services, whether they have a thousand employees or just the owner/operator, and they will come in on a regular basis to do the work as needed. It is a long-term relationship with the company, rather than with any single employee. But it's still a relationship.

Just as you would evaluate an individual before you hire them to make sure they are trustworthy and reliable, so, too, should you interview a business before you contract with them. The building you purchase will already be using vendors to do most, if not all, of the things you will need done, but never just assume they're the best fit for you. Interview them, interview other businesses that do the same kind of work, and don't ever believe someone who tells you "They're all alike." People have different values and professionalism and, inevitably, so do the companies they run.

Eventually, I ended up creating a management company, including landscaping, to keep all of the general, ongoing work in-house. As

I mentioned, I determined that five hundred units was the golden number for the most productive and efficient use of my team, and I worked to achieve that goal. You may someday decide to do the same, but until then, it makes sense to bring in contractors you trust to do much of that work.

Finally, there are professionals you need only every so often, or sometimes only in an emergency. It behooves you to meet some of those people now, before you actually need them. Talk to friends, get referrals, read online reviews, and reach out to see who might be a good fit for you. Having the number of someone who can repair the washing machines or fix the roof is priceless insurance against the inevitable problems that will arise. And whether they are employees, independent contractors, or as-needed professionals, they should all be chosen with care. They are all members of your team.

Training Your Manager

Your manager is the lynchpin of your success. If all I ever did was put in a manager whom I had personally trained, I would still have made money on my buildings. Many people hire a relative or friend as a live-in manager, and I cannot think of a worse decision. This is a business of relationships, and managers are on the front lines. Why would you want anyone less than a trained professional to represent you to your tenants?

Here are the parameters I created to outline a manager's duties and responsibilities for our properties.

Personal Appearance and Demeanor

The manager should dress professionally. They should at all times be neat and clean. Business casual is appropriate; they don't need to wear a suit, but they should never be in torn jeans and a T-shirt during working hours.

Managers should also be personable. Tenants should feel comfortable talking to them. At the same time, they need to be professional, reliable, and consistent. This, too, will help develop relationships of mutual respect between managers and tenants. It is very important that a manager respect a tenant's privacy. Being tactful and diplomatic is part of the job. They should act promptly when a tenant requests a repair or brings up a complaint or problem. Tenants need to feel they are respected and heard. At the same time, the manager should also take remedial action when tenants display unacceptable behavior. One simple, daily habit should be to walk around the complex at different times of day. Take the pulse of the property and note any unusual activity.

The manager is also in charge of collecting rents. Rent checks should be collected on or before the due date. You may have a drop box, or tenants may turn it into the manager personally, or, with online banking, some checks may arrive through the mail. Collecting rent also means filling out forms, as the manager must keep track of who has paid on time and who has not. The Appendix of this book has several sample forms that you can adapt to be filled out and stored online, but there's still something to be said for filling out simple forms by hand and scanning and sending them to the main office. If something happens to your computer system, nothing beats having actual paper backups in an old-fashioned filing cabinet.

Keep Public Areas Neat and Clean

You will have professional cleaners come in when an apartment becomes vacant; getting an apartment back to a rent-out level of cleanliness is beyond a manager's training or ability. But often your manager's duties will include basic cleaning and maintenance of public areas. Your manager should, as a matter of habit, remove any litter they find scattered around the building, including the sidewalks, stairs, mailboxes, laundry room, carport, etc. Keeping the laundry room clean, including cleaning the machines when needed and regularly emptying the lint screens and trash receptacles, would also be a regular duty. An apartment house isn't necessarily like a big office complex, where you have a full-time cleaning crew to come in daily. Things like sweeping or mopping the steps (being sure to keep safety signs posted until the stairs are completely dry) and vacuuming the common room might very well be part of their weekly to-do list.

Public Safety

A good manager needs to be proactive rather than reactive when it comes to public safety. Preventing hazardous situations by properly storing chemicals and cleaning supplies in a secure area, away from children; repairing electrical wires and outlets or railings; promptly removing things like broken glass or oil/grease—this is how to be proactive in keeping your tenants safe. Eliminate potential accidents by letting the main office know of such things as elevated tree roots or split/dead branches, loose rain gutters or ones jammed with debris, and expired or damaged fire extinguishers. Replace lightbulbs and confirm on a routine basis that lighting on walkways and stairs, as well as around the pool, remains on from dusk to dawn. Inspect the roof before winter and make sure any debris is removed.

There's really no way to give you a complete list of what your manager should check for, because every property is unique. Your weather will determine whether you need to shovel for snow, for instance—not something I've had to deal with in Southern California! Your property may or may not have a pool or a fountain or automatic gates. This is one of the reasons why it's incumbent upon you to hire a manager with common sense. You want someone who can learn by experience and is willing to take on a leadership role when it comes to safety.

Apartment Vacancies and Renting

Renting an apartment starts with someone vacating. Whenever

that happens, there are forms to fill out and steps to take, but a good manager will start by evaluating the tenant who is leaving. Are they an ideal tenant? Are they someone we would want to keep? If so, the manager should reach out to find out the reasons behind the move and, if possible, see if a win-win could be reached to keep an excellent tenant. Filling the unit isn't really that hard if you're willing to rent to anyone; finding another excellent tenant who pays on time, is respectful to other tenants, and takes excellent care of the apartment . . . that's a little harder. Keep them if you can.

However, if the tenant is, in fact, going to leave, the manager needs to be on top of it. A tenant should turn in a Thirty (30) Day Notice of Intent to Vacate form, one of the forms you will find in the Appendix, and the manager should scan and send a copy of it to your main office that same day. You want to create a sense of urgency to start filling the vacancy; do not delay letting everyone know that there will soon be an opening. After that, the manager should:

- Hang out the "For Rent" sign.
- Begin advertising the vacancy (online, with street signs, notifying a realtor if you are using one, etc.).
- Set up appointments with prospective tenants on your waiting list to view the apartment. Be sure to notify the existing tenant that you will be showing the apartment.
- Schedule an open house every weekend for as long as there is a vacancy.

I have a whole section, below, on preparing to rent the apartment, but I do want to mention a couple of other things here. One is the handoff of keys. The manager should make sure to get the keys from the tenant when they leave—not only the keys for the apartment, but also for the laundry room, mailbox, and any other space that requires a separate key. The second is that the final inspection of the apartment should be done by a professional who is NOT the manager. You want to keep the manager neutral in what might end up being a dispute between the departing tenant and your company in terms of how much of their security deposit they're getting back. Also, your manager is not an inspector by training. While they can probably see things that definitely need repairing, they cannot be expected to make the evaluation of what is normal wear-and-tear versus what more subtle issues require work. Your manager is a professional in their own realm; don't compromise their usefulness by asking them to make determinations outside of their area of expertise.

Set Managers Up for Success

Forms, many samples of which you will find in the Appendix, and directories are simple to put together and useful beyond words. Make it easy for your manager to find the emails and phone numbers of the people they will be contacting on a regular basis. Make it simple for them to gather and disseminate the information they need with forms and distribution lists. We provide every office with a directory for all maintenance contractors, a directory of our administrative team, an emergency directory, etc. Much of the information in this section comes from a 150-page manual that we put together to walk a new manager through almost every situation they will encounter. Whatever makes sense for your business, just put all the information in one place.

We also offer bonuses. For instance, we provide a manager bonus for pre-renting an apartment. We consider a unit to be pre-rented when a lease agreement is signed and the security deposit and first month's rent are collected before the former tenant has moved out. There should be no more than a week between a tenant vacating the unit and the new tenant moving in. Any repairs/cleaning will need to be accomplished in that short window. It's worth offering a manager bonus to make sure this transition runs smoothly. We also offer a bonus to managers who sign new or existing tenants to two-year leases. This is another example of a win-win. Tenants who plan to stay long-term will benefit from a two-year lease because it locks in their rent schedule. You benefit by decreasing turnover and vacancies, which eat into your cash flow. You should at least consider offering multiple lease terms (two-year, one-year, and month-to-month); doing so offers flexibility to your tenants and benefits for each of you. Offering your manager a bonus for encouraging good tenants to opt for the longer-term lease is a great way to keep the best tenants and reduce vacancy days.

Make expectations clear. Provide forms, directories, and instructions. Give your manager a reason to go the extra mile. Their success is your success.

Preparing to Rent

Marketing is everything. Successfully renting out your units also involves marketing. Tenants are shopping for the right apartment. How are they going to find yours? Once they do, how are you going to help them realize that yours is the right apartment for them?

The first hurdle is curb appeal. This is on you. Before you buy the property, you want to make sure the location is convenient for your ideal tenant. Want students? Make sure it's near a college. Want young professionals? Choose a neighborhood where they already work and live in abundance, maybe one with good public transportation and a lively nightlife. Families may like a quieter neighborhood, not too far from their jobs. See who already lives in that neighborhood and if that is, in fact, the right fit for you. Once you've purchased the property, landscape it. Make it inviting. People will only take the next step of looking at your units if the location and exterior of the property already meet their needs.

Two-sided apartment signs allow you to swivel them depending on the situation. No vacancy? The side with only the building's name and street number should face forward. The back of the sign should be displayed when you do have a vacancy, and it should include additional information on the units (one-, two-, or three-bedroom; one, one and a half, or two baths, etc.), whether or not there is a pool, and the manager's phone number. Other useful signs to keep on site are

"Open House" signs, which should be displayed by your manager on weekends when you have a vacancy. These need to be put up around the area, offering directions to potential tenants, on the morning of the open house and collected in the evening.

Make use of websites! Technology is shifting so quickly that there may be a dozen more apps/websites/social media platforms by the time you read this, so I'm not going to recommend any, but I'm sure the options will be many and varied. Make use of them. You might also have an arrangement with a real estate broker; again, this is a business of relationships. On that same note, if you have multiple buildings, make sure your managers are networking with each other. Have a way for them to keep abreast (and easily inform others) of vacancies in other buildings; a weekly, printable Vacancy Guide makes sharing the information easy. Not every unit will be right for every prospective tenant. Managers should freely recommend your other properties to prospective tenants if their property isn't a good fit. This is another reason why you want to hire personable, professional managers: they should be able to develop good relationships with each other and with anyone who walks in as a potential tenant. Your manager creates the first impression a prospective tenant will have of your property.

It's often a good idea to show the prospect the building's amenities before showing them the actual unit. Let them get a feel for the building, for what it would be like to live there. This means your manager needs to make sure the building is "show-ready" at any moment. They should be relaxed and personable, showing the prospect around the outdoor spaces (including parking spaces), pool, laundry room, and any common rooms before taking them up to the open unit. This also gives the manager time to ask some questions to find out what the prospect's criteria are. What are they looking for in terms of location? Rent schedule? Apartment size? How many people will be moving in? What is their vision of their new home?

Then it's time to show off the empty unit. "Staging" the apartment is critical. I don't mean putting in rented furniture, I mean making sure the place is clean, that it looks fresh. Every room should be free of dust and recently vacuumed. You need to make sure the electricity and water remain on; a few days before the tenant leaves, contact your utility companies to have them transferred to your business account. (Your new tenant will do something similar right before they move in; it is almost always easier to have service transferred than to have it disconnected and reconnected.) Put show towels, soap, and toilet paper in the bathrooms. Put out a bowl of fruit or a small vase of flowers. Open the curtains or blinds, and maybe spritz some air freshener before you show the apartment. Always turn on the lights. You never want a unit to feel dark or musty. Set out a card table and chairs; include pens, application forms, Open House sheets if appropriate, and any other information that might help someone deciding whether or not to lease.

If the prospective tenant decides not to fill out an application form, ask why. Some may not tell you, but others will. Try to get a sense of what about the apartment is unappealing. Some things can't be overcome; for me, if a unit has no windows at all, well, who wants to live in a box? But other times, there are either things you can do to improve the unit or there are things you can do to target the right kind of tenant, someone for whom, say, being on the third floor is a bonus (so much quieter!) and not a drawback. In any case, knowledge is power, and if your manager asks in a way that is respectful, genuinely curious, and nonjudgmental, you might get some answers. Beneficial improvements might include upgrading fixtures or appliances, installing new or hypoallergenic carpet, adding drapes or blinds, etc. You have to evaluate each suggestion and decide what will help people say yes to your units. Vacancies are extremely costly; many improvements pay for themselves by keeping the units occupied and allowing you to charge at the top of the market.

Discrimination

I hope I don't have to tell you not to discriminate against potential tenants. Unlawful housing discrimination can take many forms and there may be both federal and state laws to take into account. It is your responsibility to know the laws and communicate them to your team.

It's important for every potential tenant to be treated equally during the entire application process.

The Psychology of the Owner-Tenant Relationship

While I want you to have a good relationship with your tenants, it's important for you to establish clearly that, although they live there, you are the property's owner. This is true whether you are leasing forty units in a major complex or renting out a single-family home. How you do this is to make it clear that the burden of decision-making rests with you.

This does not mean you shouldn't listen to other people. Good ideas come from everywhere! And as the owner, you will constantly be in relationship with a wide variety of people, all of whom have a different perspective of your property: your tenants, of course, but also your employees. Your on-site manager, if you have one. Vendors, landscapers, regulators, even neighbors. Everyone sees things a little differently, and if you can be open to hearing their insights, you can often find valuable advice. The key is to listen to everyone before making a final decision. You want to be able to anticipate the possible consequences of your decisions from as many different angles as possible. This is particularly true of decisions that will have a long-term impact on the property.

You are the CEO. You need to get the best advice from everyone, make up your own mind, and be willing to change direction if events prove you were wrong. That's really the hallmark of a leader. You don't want to be badge-heavy, by which I mean that you don't want to use your power just for the sake of throwing it around. You want to really take in other people's perspectives to make the best decision, and not be so egotistical that you don't think you could ever make a mistake. I've sure made my share! But mistakes are best solved when they're first noticed and still relatively small. Problems mushroom when you ignore them, or worse, when you dig in because you can't handle the thought of having been wrong. Listen to people's concerns, let stakeholders weigh in on big decisions, try to anticipate repercussions and any problems that a new direction might engender, and make people feel heard. Just that alone can mitigate the pushback that changes always bring, even changes for the better.

Finding the Right Tenants

Your manager is the key to keeping your units occupied. This sounds obvious, but it is worth having an actual plan in place for how you are going to keep the tenants who are already there and get new ones to provide the rental income that is the key to your financial success. Your goal is to have all units rented at all times, although you should always factor in a vacancy rate of 3 percent to 5 percent when creating your budget.

Your manager is critical to your success in two ways.

1. It is almost always more cost-effective to keep the tenants you already have than to try to find new ones. If a current resident is unhappy, having a manager who can address the problem and mitigate the unhappiness can result in keeping a good tenant. The key here is to have someone who understands that fixing the leak, for example, isn't their only concern. The resident wants to feel heard; they want to feel that management is responsive to their needs. There's a certain diplomacy involved. Fixing the concrete problem is only part of resolving the situation to the resident's satisfaction.

2. The manager is usually the first person a prospective resident will seek out. When you are looking to fill empty units, the manager is the representative of your company. They should make prospects feel they would be welcomed into the building's community. Again, it's a mixture of both competence and a human touch.

You can't just rely on one person, however. There are things you could and should do to make units easier to rent. Roughly, this falls into two categories. First, use as many different ways of getting the word out as possible. Let other residents know that a unit will be coming open if they have friends who are apartment-hunting. You may have a list of prospective tenants who have inquired when you did not yet have an opening; call them. Use the Internet to spread the word by posting on your own website and in local neighborhood groups. Put out a "For Rent" sign where it can be easily seen from the sidewalk and the street. To some extent, it's a numbers game: not everyone who views the apartment will discover that the unit is right for them, but if you get enough people in the door, you will find someone who is a good fit.

Second, understand the psychology of a renter. They are someone looking for a home—not a "unit," but a "home." You are someone who provides warm, clean, safe homes. Let that be reflected when someone comes to check the place out. Think of the outside of your property like the packaging on a gift box. A well-designed landscape with colorful plants and well-maintained greenery will entice prospective residents and also command respect in the neighborhood. You want paths and entryways that are well-lit; there is a great deal of literature on how broken bulbs or windows signal that the owner doesn't care. Visible neglect can open up the property to potential vandalism and abuse by others. An inviting, well-maintained landscape and entryway can offer you pride of ownership at the same time that it signals to vendors, neighbors, and residents that this is a property to be respected.

Street appeal needs to continue once your prospective resident is inside the door. After a move-out, your first order of business should be to thoroughly clean the unit. Repaint. Clean the carpeting and the windows. People will value the apartment more if they see it as desirable from the get-go. Next, make it feel like home. The choice of paint color, carpets, and draperies can change a unit from depressing to inviting. You don't have to stage it to quite the same level as realtors selling million-dollar houses, but it's worth the effort to put colorful hand towels in the bathroom (and for goodness' sake, make sure there's toilet paper!). Put a card table and a couple of chairs in the living area and draw back the curtains to let the natural light shine in. Put a potted plant in the kitchen. Create a feeling of domesticity so that they can picture themselves happy there. In exchange, you will find the people most attracted to the unit are those who want the kind of experience you provide. These are residents who will be a good fit for you.

Just as you have expectations (for instance, that a resident will not be destructive and will pay their rent on time), so, too, do residents have expectations for their experience with you. First and foremost, they expect to be able to live their lives without hassle. They expect things to run smoothly, they expect peace and quiet, and they have a quite reasonable expectation of privacy. So long as they are in possession of the apartment, no one, including you, should seek to enter their apartment without permission. If you need to replace something, for instance, you should let them know ahead of time when the work will be done and be willing to reschedule it within reason if that date or time is inconvenient for them. This is their home. The only exception is an actual emergency requiring immediate action.

The residents will also expect the property to be well-maintained. Letting things slide—landscaping, cleaning, or anything that relates to the attractiveness of the property—is never a good idea. No one wants to feel like they're on a sinking ship. Keeping on top of regular maintenance issues is far better than waiting for things to break. Emergencies will happen. You can't plan your way out of all of them, but building into your expenditures a new hot water heater every ten years is better than sticking all your tenants with cold showers for a month while you scramble for a solution.

I always believe it's best to keep your property in top shape at all times, for a number of reasons. First, making prompt repairs and keeping up appearances increases the perceived value of living there. Sure, you may make more money in the short run by cutting expenses and deferring maintenance, but you will always lose out in the long run by not being able to keep your rent schedule at the top of the market. Neglecting appearances also means that when a unit is vacated, it'll take longer to re-rent it. Where would you rather live: someplace well-cared for or someplace where it's clear the owner couldn't care less?

Your residents judge (probably accurately) how well you will care for the inside of the property—in other words, their homes—by how well you care for the outside.

It's also difficult to predict when you will want to put the property up for sale. You may plan to keep it for decades, but life has a way of changing course. The reasons for wanting to sell range from personal situations, such as divorce, to suddenly finding your dream property on the market and needing to use your current building to finance the new purchase. Keeping up the property means that it can command top dollar no matter when you need to put it on the market. It goes beyond curb appeal to the potential buyer: you maximize your value based on your rent schedule, which is in turn maximized by having a well-maintained property.

Bad Tenants

My view of a good resident has always been pretty basic: I wanted to rent to decent people. I always tried to make them comfortable because that was the best win-win I could think of. They were comfortable and happy because I was able to provide excellent shelter for them; in return, they would tell their friends, who also tended to be very decent people. Their happiness was my success.

My definition of a bad tenant was equally simple: it was someone who destroyed the peace that good tenants deserved. Why would I want to rent to someone who was noisy or wandered around the halls drunk? Why should they ruin the experience of the other people in the building? I didn't need their rent so desperately that I was willing to risk losing everyone else by pandering to them. This is an immensely freeing realization, by the way, because having an empty unit is better than having a tenant who will drive other residents away. Other tenants might not have caused trouble, but from a financial perspective, there was no upside to having residents who were routinely late with the rent. Sometimes you can correct people by making your expectations (and any consequences for their continued actions) clear, and you end up getting along. I always wanted to befriend people, to give them a chance to be their best selves. I know it sounds naive, but I was never their boss—in fact, to some extent, I was their partner. I owned the property and I cared for it; they rented the property and they, too, cared for it. I always believed in that equality. It was a relationship I enjoyed.

That said, over the years I've had some run-ins with residents who were not a good fit. Sometimes, the solution was simple. If someone continued to violate the rules of their lease, the manager and I (and any other appropriate staff) took the time to record these violations, issued verbal warnings, issued written warnings, and, if the behavior continued, began eviction proceedings. Landlords have many regulations they need to follow, and it is important to always follow the letter of the law exactly, but there is a recourse for moving someone along who is making life difficult.

CASE STUDY

The Tenant from Hell

Every so often you will have the Tenant from Hell. That is, you will have a tenant who is disruptive on many accounts. They might be late on rent payment (or not pay rent at all) or be loud noise makers, either with their music or television blasting or constant arguing, screaming, or slamming their doors. They may break things such as windows, cause excessive holes in the wall with pictures, break blind cords, leave laundry in the washing machine or dryer for hours or days, use a parking space reserved for others, etc.

Sometimes the person will already have been in the building when you bought it; sometimes you've made a poor choice in renting to them. Mistakes happen. This is not about assigning blame. You have to deal with what you have. The question is, how do you handle the situation?

Start off by never letting the problem become personal. You want your tenants to understand that you are simply a representative of a family business, or as a corporation such as a C corporation or limited liability corporation (LLC). This isn't a personal confrontation, but rather a business situation that needs to be resolved. Avoid personal contact and demeaning insults.

Second, have written rules in place that you can make reference to. These rules should be incorporated into your rental agreement and also posted around the building as appropriate (for example, rules about leaving laundry should be posted in the laundry room, rules about noise or parties in a common room area, etc.).

Finally, pull together the tenants who are affected by the bad behavior, such as with a signed petition. You will still be the one to take action, but it's good to have the backing of your other tenants.

Here's a perfect example from one of my buildings. We had one such problem tenant; he was a single man with two children. The tenant and his children were always loud, both in and out of their apartment. There was a lot of noise, yelling, and slamming of doors at all hours. The children would annoy other children by splashing them in the pool and chalking inappropriate words on the sidewalk. The family would leave laundry in the laundry room, either in the machines or all over the folding areas, for hours or days. When you have many communal areas (laundry/pool/playground), it's impossible to avoid other people, and their behavior made interacting with them—and therefore, taking advantage of the amenities that were included in the rent—unpleasant. Many of my other tenants were complaining about their bad behavior and wanted them out of the building.

A response plan was put into place. First, we let Dad and children know they misspelled a word on the sidewalk; we requested they clean it up. We posted a sign in the laundry room: "Laundry wet or dry left in the machine past one hour should be removed and placed in a basket." And then we enforced that across the board. You want to be careful—you never want to single out one tenant; any rule you make has to apply to everyone. But most people have no problem following rules that exist to make the experience better for everyone. Troublemaking tenants, however, will almost always decide the rules don't apply to them and will ignore them or willfully break them.

In this case, the tenant didn't pay his rent on time. He was fined a late payment fee (again, a rule we had for everyone), and he refused to pay it. At this point, we filed a Three-Day Notice, which was legally the next step for us in the eviction process (this may vary depending on where you are; you should always know what the laws are protecting tenants and landlords in your particular neck of the woods). Once again, he refused to pay. We filed with the court and the judge gave an Order for Eviction. The Tenant from Hell was forced to move out.

Every situation is unique. What matters is that you remain

professional and enforce rules fairly throughout your buildings, and remember that your good tenants also have the right to a peaceful home.

You will need to make sure you understand the eviction procedure in your state, but here are some steps we go through in Los Angeles County:

- Preparing the eviction notice is the first step. The notice should be served personally if possible.
- The tenant has until the notice expires to comply with the notice; for instance, a Three-Day Notice might be served if the tenant hasn't paid their rent by the first of the month. They have those three days to remedy the situation by, in fact, paying the rent. If they don't, it's time for an attorney to prepare an eviction complaint and file it with the court.
- The summons will be served on the tenant. The tenant may file an answer at this point, which will lead to a trial date, but if they don't, a default judgment may be issued. If there is a trial, a trial judgment will be issued. Assuming it's in your favor, the next thing that happens is that the attorneys will forward a writ to the sheriff.
- The sheriff will arrange with the manager to schedule the eviction.

Is this difficult? Time consuming? Unpleasant? Yes to all of these things. It is also necessary. You can't continue to provide homes to people if any portion of your tenants refuse to pay you.

CASE STUDY

When Tenants Set up an Adversarial Relationship

At one point, I had a property that was rent-controlled. The law allowed for me to increase the rent by a small

---

amount, with proper notification to tenants, and I did so. One of the tenants objected. Not only that, but he also organized with several other tenants who all decided they would refuse to pay the increase in rent. Their rationale, as I understand it, was that I owned several buildings, so I must be rich and therefore didn't need the extra money that the increase in rent would bring. They made no attempt to see the value of what I provided for them or how much it might cost me to maintain it to the standard of living they enjoyed. They wanted to flex their power and simply refused to pay.

The thing you should know about me is that I have always been a rule-follower. I used to work as an auditor for the IRS. I am an expert when it comes to knowing the laws and following the spirit as well as the letter. I believe in them; I believe that rules and laws exist so that we have a level playing field and a recourse for making sure other people stay honest. I understand that not everyone else will follow the rules. However, from my work as an auditor and also as a banker, where I was in charge of bringing down delinquency rates, my stance has always been, look, here's a problem that we need to solve together. How can we work together to make sure that, for instance, you are following the tax codes? Or that you can repay your loan? It often involves some level of reframing the past and moving forward with a clean slate.

As an approach to dealing with situations that need to be altered, this "we're moving forward together" perspective has served me well. However, in this case, with the residents who refused to pay the rent increase, it did not work. The ringleader was, in my opinion, in it for the sense of power it gave him. He dug in and so did his followers. After several months of impasse, I served them eviction notices for nonpayment of rent, and that just fueled them further. They weren't planning to pay and they weren't planning to leave.

So I took them to court.

I won, too. Of course I did. That thing about being a believer in rules? What it means is that I am scrupulous about following the rules myself. I knew what the law allowed and I followed all the appropriate guidelines to a tee, and the judge had no qualms about ruling for me. It was (if they had been clear-eyed enough to see it) the only possible outcome. In any case, I won, and they had to move out. Several of them actually asked to stay even though the rent would no longer be bound by the rent-controlled agreement they had initially scorned. I could charge them three times the amount they had been refusing to pay these last few months. But I didn't want them there. They had caused me time and money and a court date, but most of all, they had disrespected the effort I put into creating and maintaining a building they could be happy to call home. I could never have the same relationship with them that I'd had before all of this. Even though it resulted in several empty units, the vacancies were temporary. For me, it was worth it to not have to deal with them anymore.

The lessons here are, first, to be sure you understand the local laws governing apartment complexes, rents, zoning, and anything else that might impact your building. You don't need to be a lawyer, but as a businessperson, you must understand contracts. A lease is a contract between you and your tenant; it is a legally binding document. Educate yourself. Local ordinances are also binding and it's always to your advantage to understand and adhere to them. When disputes occur (and they will, although I hope not at quite this level for you), understanding the laws, expectations, and appropriate steps to take is the first line of defense against destructive or abusive tenants.

Second, your reasonable tenants deserve a place to live that is free from the noise, destruction, and outright malignancy of certain other people. You can't be afraid to take on the bullies because, as the owner, it is your role to make sure the rest of your tenants can live in peace. If you don't, you will find the good tenants leaving in droves, no matter how freshly painted the hallways may be, and the value of your property will sink. So long as you behave toward everyone in a professional, appropriate, and lawful manner, you can maintain the kind of environment you would like to live in yourself.

And that is the real secret to management success.

Final Thoughts

I hope that reading this book has given you a lot of ideas, maybe opened up your eyes to the ways in which apartment house ownership can give you security, satisfaction, and the opportunity to build generational wealth. But there's a next step to it, which is actually going out there, looking at properties, getting your financing together, and eventually making an offer.

Suddenly, things get very real.

Until you make an offer, everything you do is just an exercise. It can be fun, it can be energizing, but you may not fully process everything until the day arrives to make the offer. I call this "reality shock." Suddenly, you'll feel the urge to double-check your resources. Your brain will start spinning with all the things that can go wrong. You may even want to back out. Just understand that the fear is normal. You're about to put a lot of money on the line. I'd be worried about you if you weren't a little concerned.

There comes a time in your life when you have to make a decision: will I take action or will I stand pat? And look, it's your life—you will ultimately make all your own decisions. But I can at least give you a peek at what I believe the future holds either way.

First of all, you can choose not to act. This plays out in different ways. The worst way is you telling yourself the time isn't right, that you'll revisit property ownership next year, that you'll read another book, take another class, think about it, talk about it just a little more . . . those are all lies you tell yourself so that you won't have to feel bad in the moment. You think that by putting off the decision-making, you will never have to confront your feelings of fear or uncertainty. The brain hates to be uncertain! Instead, you will tell yourself that you'll make the decision later, rather than admitting that by not making a decision now, you are in fact *making the decision* to not move forward.

This is the worst thing you can do.

Ultimately, this stalling and lying to yourself about your intentions eats away at your own sense of integrity. It leads to massive feelings of regret down the line; people often berate themselves for not taking action. "I should have" or "I could have" are thoughts that can eat away at your soul. Do yourself a favor and really look at your ambitions and desires and temperament now. Make a decision.

I'm not saying that your decision has to be to buy an apartment house. Far from it. Owning and managing an apartment house is a life-changing responsibility. Not everyone has the stamina to stay the course. I have friends who have bought apartment houses and then decided it wasn't right for them. I have another friend who knew he was just in it for the short term: at my suggestion, he bought a house near his daughter's campus when she went away to college. She found roommates to share it with, their rent checks covered the mortgage, my friend saved on housing costs, and he made a couple of thousand reselling the house after she graduated. He had no desire to be a provider of shelter long-term. But short-term? It was a win-win.

Finally, I have a friend who read my other books and decided that, nope, nothing about apartment ownership or management sounded like what he wanted to do with his life. He owns his own home, he has other investments, he has a safety net of savings, and he's thought through what he's going to do when he retires. He's set. Most of all, he's happy. He does not have the same ambitions I have, and while I admit that I may not be able to understand his choice, who cares? It's his life. And he was honest with himself now, which means no regrets later.

What may be holding you back is a fear of buyer's remorse—in other words, you're afraid of what might happen if you *do* take action.

It's the opposite of the fear of missing out; here, you're afraid of being wrong. Of failing. Okay, let's look at that. What does that mean?

It could mean losing all your money in the deal. That's not impossible, but it isn't easy to do, either, because when you're buying an apartment house, these complexes have a built-in income stream. I mentioned that when I bought my first one, I stretched myself pretty thin financially, but I never touched the equity in my own house. I knew that if things went sideways, selling my house would give me enough money to be able to keep the apartment complex and we could live there. That's not the same as losing everything, because with time, I knew I could make a go of it. The property value might go down in a correction, but I was holding it for the long term. Panic is never a good choice. I knew that eventually, the property value would increase—and "eventually" was a matter of a few years, not decades. Meanwhile, my family would have a roof over their heads, and we would have rent monies coming in. And I didn't quit my day job, not for years. I had a solid backup plan (and plenty of life insurance) that protected both my family and our most important investment, which was the apartment complex. I never needed to use Plan B, but having it in place made it almost impossible to fail.

I have "failed" in the sense that other apartment complexes were poor investments—well, one other. I treaded water with it for several years and then had to sell the property at a loss. Complete failure, right? Wrong. I made enough money to keep it going for a few years, I learned a lot about what didn't work that proved invaluable later on, I recouped a good chunk of my investment, and, again, I had a Plan B—this time, it was the income I could count on from my other properties. Even when I did make a mistake, I was never on the verge of my family living on the street. It is always worth creating a safety net, that Plan B, because having a safety net is the very thing that can give you the confidence you need to take the leap.

Your greatest resources are within you. You need the will to succeed. It is a powerful resource. Success is never a straight line; invariably, there will be times when the economy softens or regulations seem insurmountable, or even when a litigious resident goes after you. But there will be problems to overcome no matter what you invest in. It's up to you to decide which set of problems you're willing to encounter in order to make your financial dreams come true. I believe that investment in apartment houses can be a tremendous source of prosperity. It certainly has been for me.

And it's been good for others as well. Just last month, I was talking to the guy who cleans the pool at my house, and I asked him, "Hey, what do they say about the Barbera family?" And he told me.

"Oh," he said, "they love you! When I retire, I'm going to move into a Barbera-managed apartment."

And he couldn't have said anything I would want to hear more. Success is all about creating a feeling: through the manager, through the company's policies of maintenance, through service to residents, through bringing great residents into the property, you create the feeling of peace and harmony that people want to live in.

I live for the long run. Playing by the rules, treating people fairly, and exercising patience can lead to success. You are not alone in wanting financial security and peace of mind, or in wanting to better your lot in life. It's the American way. I believe that providing excellent housing improves the lives of those around you while at the same time building a financial legacy you can leave to your children and to their children. There is no greater satisfaction than to be able to look back on your life and say, "Yes. It was hard. It took courage and integrity and sacrifice. But I did it."

I wish you every success.

APPENDIX

SAMPLE FORMS

How to Use the Sample Forms

The following pages contain sample forms to help you see what kinds of forms you need and what they might look like. These forms are meant to help you build your own forms and processes to make sure your buildings run smoothly.

I did not include a lease. Why? Because I am not a lawyer, and because laws vary depending on your location, and they change over time. I don't want you to think that what I provide will work as a one-size-fits-all, because it definitely won't. But not to worry—when you purchase an apartment building, they will already have their standard lease in place for you to use as a template. You should have your own lawyer look it over to make sure it still covers current laws and best practices. (As I mentioned, I don't love lawyers being in on negotiations, but I absolutely recommend having lawyers advise you on contracts. And a lease is a contract.) We offer three different types of leases: two-year, one-year, and month-to-month. I believe offering your tenants some flexibility is preferable, but you will decide what works best for you and the people you seek to serve.

For the other forms, again, adapt them to work for your building. If a form references the lease or a local law, I have indicated that in brackets; you should fill in the appropriate language from your own situation.

Finally, there is no one right answer for any given form, or even for which forms you may use. These have worked for us, but I expect you will find yourself creating new forms for specific situations. That's as it should be. Educate yourself about local, state, and national laws, as well as best practices, on an ongoing basis. You can always improve and finesse to create a business that works for you.

VACANCY SIGN-IN SHEET

It will be advantageous for you to have prospects provide you with the information below when they come to view the apartment—and advantageous for them as well. They may not move quickly enough to get the unit currently open, or the time may not be right, but by having their information, you can let them know when another unit opens up.

WEEK OF _____   BUILDING _____

OPEN HOUSE DATE _____   TIME _____

DATE	NAME	PHONE/EMAIL	REFERRED BY

NEW TENANT INFORMATION

[Include your office address and email here, so the tenant has a way to reach you directly in case of issues with the manager.]

NAME(S) OF **ALL** RESIDENTS

_____

APARTMENT ADDRESS _____ APT _____
CITY _____ ZIP _____   _____
PARKING SPACE _____   _____
_____

THE FOLLOWING INFORMATION SHOULD BE USEFUL IN ARRANGING THE
SERVICES YOU WILL NEED.

MANAGER'S NAME   APT   PHONE
ELECTRIC CO   _____ ____ PHONE _____
GAS CO _____ PHONE _____
TELEPHONE CO   PHONE _____
CREDIT CHECK: _____   _____
CREDIT CHECK FEE FOR EACH ADULT $_____
TOTAL RECEIVED $_____
SECURITY DEPOSIT AND FIRST MONTH'S RENT
KEY DEPOSIT: DATE _____   AMOUNT $_____
PET DEPOSIT: DATE_____   AMOUNT $_____
SECURITY DEPOSIT: DATE _____   AMOUNT $_____
TOTAL DEPOSITS (ANY DEPOSIT MAY BE USED FOR ANY CHARGEABLE ITEM):
                                         $_____
FIRST MONTH'S RENT: DATE_____   AMOUNT $_____

MANAGER _____ DATE _____
TENANT _____ DATE _____
TENANT _____ DATE _____

[This side to be filled out by manager.]

NAMES OF ALL OCCUPANTS	WORK PHONE	HOME OR CELL PHONE

EMERGENCY CONTACT NAMES	ADDRESS	CELL PHONE

	VEHICLE 1	VEHICLE 2	VEHICLE 3
MAKE			
LICENSE PLATE			
YEAR			
COLOR			

PARKING SPACE(S)	STORAGE SPACE

Please note each city may have different street parking rules for daytime and night-time parking. It is the tenant's responsibility to know and abide by the city rules. No visitor parking is permitted on premises. Any unauthorized parking will be enforced by towing the vehicle; the tenant will be responsible for any related cost.

MANAGER _____ DATE _____

TENANT _____ DATE _____

TENANT _____ DATE _____

[This side to be filled out by tenant(s).]

MAINTENANCE FORMS

Repair Request

Tenants would fill out a Repair Request Form and turn it into the manager. In fact, one of the manager's responsibilities was to make sure all tenants were given several Repair Request Forms when they moved in and periodically thereafter. Ideally, the tenant would provide detailed information about the problem, which can often save time, money, and a lot of frustration. Occasionally, the forms would be filled out by the manager themselves. If the repair was an emergency, we would expect the manager to call the main office immediately so that we could get someone out there as soon as possible. If it was not an emergency, repairs were batched and performed once a week (see below). The original Repair Request Forms were bundled up and turned into the main office with the rent checks once a month.

Weekly Summary of Maintenance Requests

The way I set up my properties, each apartment complex had a weekly service day when repair people would take care of whatever needed fixing on that particular property. Obviously, if an emergency repair was needed, someone would go out immediately. But for the property itself, many repairs could wait a few days. Repair Request Forms would be gathered up the day before a property's weekly service day, and then the manager would fill out a single form summarizing all requests, which they would then forward to our office. In my day, it was via fax, but today it would almost certainly be by email. Our office would, in turn, schedule the appropriate professionals to go out the following day to handle all repairs.

The manager was expected to be present when the service professionals were scheduled to arrive, but that was not always possible. If the manager was unable to be present, we used a lock box, but it was still the manager's responsibility to make sure the repair people could get into the building and the unit.

REPAIR REQUEST FORM

DAY	ADDRESS
DATE	UNIT #
TENANT NAME	ROOOM(S) OF REPAIR

Please explain FULLY the repair needed. Indicate the exact room, fixtures, make or model, type of repair, and any damage that has resulted:

[Note that the manager must check the tenant's complaint to confirm the repair request, cause, and urgency.]

YOU HAVE MY PERMISSION TO ENTER MY APARTMENT AS SOON AS POSSIBLE. I MAY BE REACHED AT THE FOLLOWING PHONE NUMBERS:

DAY:	EVENING:
SIGNATURE	DATE

REPAIR NOTICE MUST BE RECEIVED BEFORE MAINTENANCE IS SCHEDULED.

Please make sure a signature and phone number are on each Repair Request Form.

WEEKLY SUMMARY OF MAINTENANCE REQUESTED BY MANAGER

BUILDING _____   DATE _____

MANAGER: PLEASE REMEMBER TO PLACE KEYS IN THE LOCK BOX

MANAGER

*	APARTMENT NUMBER	REPAIR REQUEST DATE	EXPLANATION OF REPAIR	**

SERVICE PROVIDER

DATE	TIME IN	TIME OUT	TOTAL TIME	COST OF SUPPLIES

MANAGER'S SERVICE DATES:

STEPS _____   LAUNDRY ROOM _____

LIGTHTS _____   OTHER _____

* INDICATE Y/N IF REPAIR NEEDED WAS CAUSED BY TENANT NEGLIGENCE   ** MARK C = IF COMPLETED OR I = INCOMPLETE

ON-THE-SPOT RECOGNITION FORM

Impressed by a job well-done?
Please let us know who on our team is going above and beyond!

Name of Team Member: _____

Area of Service: _____

Please describe the noteworthy performance or service:

_____

_____

_____

_____

Building _____ Apt ____ Date _____

Tenant's Name _____

Signature _____

THREE (3) DAY NOTICE TO PAY RENT OR QUIT

To_____ and all other tenants in possession of
the premises described as:

_____

Street Address   Apartment

_____

City   County   State   Zip Code

PLEASE TAKE NOTICE that the rent is now due and payable on the above-described premises which you currently hold and occupy. Your rental account is now delinquent in the amount itemized as follows:

The current monthly rent is $ _____

Rent for above Rental Period: $ _____
Less partial payment of: $ _____
BALANCE DUE: $ _____

You are hereby required to pay said rent in full or to remove from and deliver up possession of the above-described premises within three (3) days or legal proceedings will be instituted against you to recover possession of said premises, to declare the forfeiture of the Lease or Rental Agreement under which you occupy said premises and to recover rents and damages together with court costs and attorney fees, according to the terms of your Lease or Rental Agreement. Payment of this notice shall be made to Manager, Phone # _____, Address _____ _____ , and, if delivering payment in person, payment shall be made during the hours of _____.

Dated this _____ day of _____, 20____.

_____

Owner/Agent

IMPORTANT! ONLY CASHIER'S CHECK OR MONEY ORDER FOR THE FULL AMOUNT DUE WILL BE ACCEPTED AS PAYMENT OF RENT. *As required by law, you are hereby notified that a negative credit report reflecting on your credit history may be submitted to a credit reporting agency if you fail to fulfill the terms of your credit obligations.*

THIRTY (30) DAY NOTICE OF INTENT TO VACATE

Please be advised that the undersigned intends to vacate the premises located at:

_____
Street Address   Apartment

_____
City   County   State   Zip Code

I intend to move on DATE: _____ being fully aware of the [INSERT APPROPRIATE LAW] which states that a 30-day written notice must be given, and that rent shall be due and payable up to and including the date of termination.

Reason for Move: _____

_____

_____

Forwarding Address: _____

_____

Telephone: Day _____   Evening _____

[I recommend that you insert here the appropriate sections of your lease regarding 1) the termination of the lease contract, 2) the right of your manager to enter the apartment for purposes of repair and/or showing the unit, 3) any language outlining the consequences of them preventing the apartment from being shown, and 4) that the security deposit is *not* to be used as the last month's rent. It's better to quote the exact language of the lease here rather than just "reminding" them because, in fact, these are written, contractual agreements. Legal language carries weight.]

Wear and Tear

Ordinary Wear: This is considered normal use; however this does not include anything that has been scratched or marred, hole spots, tears, stains, rips, or broken or missing items.

General Cleaning

Trash, litter, furniture, clothing, papers, personal items, or anything brought into the apartment or parking areas by the tenant need to be removed from the property.

Additional Specific Cleaning Needed

A. Window coverings, drapes, blinds, and shower enclosures must be cleaned without smudges, streaks, or mineral deposits. Screens must be free of dust. Drapes must be free of dust, stains, and wrinkles. Both sides of windows and window coverings must be clean.

B. All fixtures including tubs, showers, faucets, and light fixtures must be clean.

C. All appliances including stoves, refrigerators (inside and outside), air conditioners (filters), wall heaters, faucets, and showerheads must be clean.

D. All flooring: a general cleaning of steps, hardwood floors, linoleum/tile including areas under appliances, as well as carpets (including closet areas) and garage floors must all be free of spots, stains, marring, and dust.

E. Garage areas must be free of personal items, grease, dust, and locks.

It is always recommended that the tenant attend to general cleaning; specific cleaning, however, is different. The tenant has a choice of taking care of the specific cleaning or having the landlord hire professionals. Professional cleaning will be charged to the tenant if not performed satisfactorily; the professionals may charge as much in this case as they would if the tenant had not attempted the cleaning in the first place. In most cases, the tenant has neither the time nor the experience or inclination to bring the apartment back to its original condition.

Deposit Refund Policy

At the termination of your tenancy, your apartment will be inspected by the manager only as a Preliminary Inspection. When the apartment is completely vacated, it will be the Independent Inspector who determines the necessary corrective actions for apartment restoration to the apartment's original condition. After receiving your Itemized Disposition form, you may request copies of all invoices if request is made in a timely manner.

TENANT _____ DATE _____
TENANT _____ DATE _____
MANAGER _____ DATE _____

This form must be signed by all parties in each other's presence on the same date.

Reference Data by Manager

Date Manager Received Notice _____ Date Sent to Office _____
Occupancy Period: From _____ To _____

Payment Record:
On time _____ Late _____ Non-Sufficient Funds _____ Evicted _____
House Rules Followed: Yes _____ No _____
Notices Issued _____
Apartment Condition (Preliminary Inspection):
Excellent _____ Fair _____ Poor _____

MOVE-OUT FORM

Fill out this form **immediately** after the tenant moves out. Do not discuss with tenant. Please fill out completely, no blank lines. Scan and send to the office the day the tenant moves out.

Building_____ Apt___ Tenant _____

Forwarding Address _____

Dates:

Notice Given _____ Moved Out _____ Lease Expires _____

Did tenant stay past 30-day notice: Y or N

   How many extra days? ____ x $_____ x 2 = _____

                    Days   Daily Rate   Total Charge

Did tenant obstruct from showing apartment? Y or N

Dates: _____

Current Rent: $_____ Rent Owed: $_____

Security Deposit: $_____

Key(s) Returned: Door ___ Laundry Room ___ Mailbox ___

       Security Gate ___ Remote ___

Indicate number of holes that need patching: _____

Anything missing/broken/damaged? _____

_____

_____

Personal items left behind: _____

_____

Date New Tenant expected to move in: _____

New Rental Rate: $_____

continued on following page

PRELIMINARY INSPECTION

KITCHEN	BATHS	1	2	BEDROOMS	M	O	O	LIV	DIN	OUTSIDE	MISC.	
SINK										RAILING		
STOVE										STAIRS		
DRAIN BOARD										DOOR		
CUPBOARDS										WALL		
FRIDGE										PKG AREA		
FLOOR												

Further clarification: _____

_____

M = Main Bedroom   O = Other _____   *O = Other* _____

Manager _____   Date _____

ACKNOWLEDGMENTS

This book would not have been possible without the help of Karen Richardson. With the reorganizing and rewriting by Laura Brenan, the book came alive. Thanks to my mother for inspiring me and constantly reminding that "Life is a bowl of cherries," to my wife Bernice for always standing behind me, and to my children Ann, John, and Pat for giving me years of support. Along the way, many people cooperated and were proud of me, which overshadowed the envious people.

About the Author

Robert Barbera is proud of his immigrant parents. They taught him the value of hard work and the importance of family. He made his first stock investment in 1954, only four years out of high school, and bought his first building in 1961. Through hard work, dedication, focus, and the support of his family, he now has 500 units and multiple subsidiary companies, making real estate the cornerstone of his success.

Throughout his life, Robert has built wealth not just for himself and his family, but for many other people in fields as diverse as restaurants, car dealerships, and the financial industry. He launched The Barbera Foundation in 1994 and has donated his time, expertise, and financial resources to many worthy organizations, including Pepperdine University, Thomas Aquinas College, and the California State University system.

Robert was lucky in love, having had a happy, forty-five-year marriage to his late wife, Bernice, and finding love a second time around with Josephine, whom he married in 2003. He is the father of three wonderful children, Ann, John, and Patricia, and the grandfather of seven.

The Mentoris Project represents a piece of Robert's legacy. It connects his past, his parents, his children, and the future by honoring the achievements of Italians and Italian-Americans, by sharing his expertise to help people create wealth and make the most of their assets, and by publishing inspirational books. Learn more at https://www.mentoris-project.org

ALSO FROM THE MENTORIS PROJECT

America's Forgotten Founding Father
A Novel Based on the Life of Filippo Mazzei
by Rosanne Welch, PhD

A. P. Giannini—Il Banchiere di Tutti
di Francesca Valente

A. P. Giannini—The People's Banker
by Francesca Valente

The Architect Who Changed Our World
A Novel Based on the Life of Andrea Palladio
by Pamela Winfrey

At Last
A Novel Based on the Life of Harry Warren
by Stacia Raymond

A Boxing Trainer's Journey
A Novel Based on the Life of Angelo Dundee
by Jonathan Brown

Breaking Barriers
A Novel Based on the Life of Laura Bassi
by Jule Selbo

Building Heaven's Ceiling
A Novel Based on the Life of Filippo Brunelleschi
by Joe Cline

Building Wealth
From Shoeshine Boy to Real Estate Magnate
by Robert Barbera

Building Wealth 101
How to Make Your Money Work for You
by Robert Barbera

Character is What Counts
A Novel Based on the Life of Vince Lombardi
by Jonathan Brown

Christopher Columbus: His Life and Discoveries
by Mario Di Giovanni

Dark Labyrinth
A Novel Based on the Life of Galileo Galilei
by Peter David Myers

Defying Danger
A Novel Based on the Life of Father Matteo Ricci
by Nicole Gregory

Desert Missionary
A Novel Based on the Life of Father Eusebio Kino
by Nicole Gregory

The Divine Proportions of Luca Pacioli
A Novel Based on the Life of Luca Pacioli
by W.A.W. Parker

The Dream of Life
A Novel Based on the Life of Federico Fellini
by Kate Fuglei

Dreams of Discovery
A Novel Based on the Life of the Explorer John Cabot
by Jule Selbo

The Embrace of Hope
A Novel Based on the Life of Frank Capra
by Kate Fuglei

The Faithful
A Novel Based on the Life of Giuseppe Verdi
by Collin Mitchell

Fermi's Gifts
A Novel Based on the Life of Enrico Fermi
by Kate Fuglei

First Among Equals
A Novel Based on the Life of Cosimo de' Medici
by Francesco Massaccesi

The Flesh and the Spirit
A Novel Based on the Life of St. Augustine of Hippo
by Sharon Reiser and Ali A. Smith

God's Messenger
A Novel Based on the Life of Mother Frances X. Cabrini
by Nicole Gregory

Grace Notes
A Novel Based on the Life of Henry Mancini
by Stacia Raymond

Harvesting the American Dream
A Novel Based on the Life of Ernest Gallo
by Karen Richardson

Humble Servant of Truth
A Novel Based on the Life of Thomas Aquinas
by Margaret O'Reilly

The Judicious Use of Intangibles
A Novel Based on the Life of Pietro Belluschi
by W.A.W. Parker

Leonardo's Secret
A Novel Based on the Life of Leonardo da Vinci
by Peter David Myers

Little by Little We Won
A Novel Based on the Life of Angela Bambace
by Peg A. Lamphier, PhD

The Making of a Prince
A Novel Based on the Life of Niccolò Machiavelli
by Maurizio Marmorstein

A Man of Action Saving Liberty
A Novel Based on the Life of Giuseppe Garibaldi
by Rosanne Welch, PhD

Marconi and His Muses
A Novel Based on the Life of Guglielmo Marconi
by Pamela Winfrey

Music's Guiding Hand
A Novel Inspired by the Life of Guido d'Arezzo
by Kingsley Day

No Person Above the Law
A Novel Based on the Life of Judge John J. Sirica
by Cynthia Cooper

The Pirate Prince of Genoa
A Novel Based on the Life of Admiral Andrea Doria
by Maurizio Marmorstein

Relentless Visionary: Alessandro Volta
by Michael Berick

Retire and Refire
Simple Financial Strategies to Navigate Your Best Years with Ease
by Robert Barbera

Ride Into the Sun
A Novel Based on the Life of Scipio Africanus
by Patric Verrone

Rita Levi-Montalcini
Pioneer & Ambassador of Science
by Francesca Valente

Saving the Republic
A Novel Based on the Life of Marcus Cicero
by Eric D. Martin

The Seven Senses of Italy: La Luna di Miele
by Nicole Gregory

Sinner, Servant, Saint
A Novel Based on the Life of St. Francis of Assisi
by Margaret O'Reilly

Soldier, Diplomat, Archaeologist
A Novel Based on the Bold Life of Louis Palma di Cesnola
by Peg A. Lamphier, PhD

The Soul of a Child
A Novel Based on the Life of Maria Montessori
by Kate Fuglei

What a Woman Can Do
A Novel Based on the Life of Artemisia Gentileschi
by Peg A. Lamphier, PhD

The Witch of Agnesi
A Novel Based on the Life of Maria Agnesi
by Eric D. Martin

For more information on these titles and the Mentoris Project, please visit
www.mentorisproject.org

www.ingramcontent.com/pod-product-compliance
Lightning Source LLC
Chambersburg PA
CBHW030511210326
41597CB00013B/870

* 9 7 8 1 9 4 7 4 3 1 5 4 6 *